DAYS OF LONELINESS

DAYS
OF
LONELINESS

By

AUGUST STRINDBERG

Translated from the Swedish

by

ARVID PAULSON

PHAEDRA INC. PUBLISHERS

49 Park Avenue, New York, N.Y. 10016

Phaedra Inc. Publishers
49 Park Avenue
New York, N.Y. 10016

This translation is dedicated to
Walter A. Berendsohn

PREFACE

Having suffered through his so-called Inferno crisis, while living abroad in the 1890's and being at the brink of madness, August Strindberg returned to his native land with improved health and settled down in the university town of Lund. In 1899 he moved to Stockholm, where he met Harriet Bosse, who became his third and last wife. After they had separated, he remained for a while a lonely recluse, then took up old friendships and joined in revelry with them. But this companionship soon grew dull and purposeless to him and he again withdrew from any association with people, went out rarely, and for long periods of time saw no one. What he experienced and, with the aid of binoculars, observed from his fifth floor windows, overlooking the surrounding landscape and the inlet from the sea, he recounts in DAYS OF LONELINESS: sad happenings and humorous ones that he wove into dramatic episodes in play and novel and short story.

Written and published in 1903, *Days Of Loneliness* was brought out under the title of *Ensam* (Alone). Containing a series of observations and meditations on human happiness and grief, frailties and vanities, Strindberg paints a canvas filled with nostalgic episodes of life in the capital of Sweden at the turn of the nineteenth century. Commenting on his experiences and observations with a sixth sense, the great Swedish writer is throughout interesting and fascinating, as well as penetrating in his depiction of character. Critics have accorded it a high place among August Strindberg's writings.

---

* The diacritical mark for the Swedish sound of *o* (*a* with a ring over it) being unavailable, a number of words, mainly proper names, are thus of necessity printed without any mark over the *a*. A.P.

DAYS OF LONELINESS

I

After spending ten years in the provinces I am back in my native city and am now sitting at table eating dinner with my old friends. We are all of us more or less in our fifties; the younger ones among us have passed forty, or are about that age. It surprises us that we show no sign of having aged since we last met. A little gray in the beard and at the temples can be noticed here and there, of course; but then there are some who have grown younger since we last saw one another. And these confess that a curious change took place in their lives when they reached forty. They felt old, and thought that their years were approaching the end. They discovered ailments which were non-existent; the upper parts of their arms felt stiff, and they had difficulty getting into their overcoats. Everything seemed old and worn to them; everything was recapitulation, an eternal repetition of the very same things. The younger generation pushed forward threateningly and paid no attention to the attainments of their elders. The most disagreeable thing of all was that the young made precisely the same discoveries that we had made. And what was worse, they put forward antiquated views as if they had never been thought of before.

However, while we were talking about remembrances—which were the remembrances of our youth—we sank back into time, literally living over again our past, and found ourselves twenty years back in time, so that one of us suddenly wondered if such a thing as time really existed.

—"That has already been cleared up by Kant," a philosopher among us enlightened the group.

—"Time is merely our way of perceiving and interpreting the present," came from another.

—"Exactly. I have come to the same conclusion. For when I

recall little happenings of forty-five years ago, they stand out as clearly as if they had taken place yesterday. And what happened in my childhood is as close to me as if I had experienced it a year ago," said still another one.

This led to a debate as to whether all those present had had similar ideas and experiences throughout life. A septuagenarian —the only one in the gathering whom we looked upon as an old man—remarked that he did not feel old at all. (He had not long before re-married and had a child in the cradle.) After this precious piece of intelligence we felt as if we were mere boys; and the tone of the conversation became actually adolescent.

It is true that I had noticed when we first met that my friends had not changed much, and this had surprised me. But I had also observed that they did not smile as easily as before and that they exercised a certain cautiousness when they spoke. They had all discovered the power and value of the spoken word. While life had not modified or softened their opinions and judgments, their prudence and common sense had with the years taught them that words once uttered had a way of coming back at one. They had also learned that people do not speak in whole tones only, but that—in order to express an opinion of a person somewhat less ambiguously—one has to resort to half-tones. And now the arguments broke loose. . . . Words were not chosen too carefully, and no respect was shown for opinions. All went back to their old ways and set off in a wild run-away. But it was fun.

Then there was a pause—several pauses. And after that, an uncomfortable silence. Those who had done the most talking were gripped by a feeling of oppression, as if they had been gabbling their heads off. They became conscious of the fact that during the past ten years each one of them had, unbeknownst to the others, found new companions, unknown different interests had come between, and that those who had spoken freely had bumped up against submerged reefs, had tugged at strings, trampled down defenses. All this they could have noticed if they had seen the glances with which their old friends armed themselves for resistance and defense, those twingings and twitchings about the mouth, with the lips hiding a suppressed word.

When they now rose from the table, it was as if the newly spun threads had been pulled apart. The mood and animation were broken, everyone was on the defensive and buttoned himself up. But since they had to say something, they came with mere phrases; and this was evidenced in their eyes, which did not keep step with their words, and by the smiles which were out of tune with the glances.

It turned out to be an insufferably long drawn-out evening. Attempts were made, individually and by groups, to revive old memories, but failed. Out of sheer stupidity one asked about matters which one should have left alone. For example: "How is your brother Herman nowadays?" (A meaningless question, tossed out as an answer to something of no interest to the one who asked.) The group is depressed. "Oh, thank you—his condition is about the same—no improvement in sight."

—"Improvement? He has been sick, then?"

—"Yes. . . . Didn't you know?"

One in the group throws himself between them and saves the unfortunate brother from having to acknowledge that Herman is mentally ill.

Or a question such as this: "Well, why is it that we don't ever see your wife?" . . . She was getting a divorce.

Or one like this: "Your son is grown now, isn't he? Has he graduated yet?"—He was the family's prodigal son. In brief, the continuity in our friendly, intimate association was disrupted, and finally broken. But we had all experienced the seriousness of life and, in any case, we were no longer boys. . . .

When we finally parted outside the entrance, we felt the necessity of bidding a hasty good-bye. We did not, as we formerly used to do, repair to a café to prolong the conviviality. The memories of youth had not, in short, had the refreshing effect that we had expected. And the past was, of course, the soil in which the present was rooted; and the growth had already been seared, had withered, was now bereft of life and beginning to grow moldy.

And it became apparent that the conversation had ceased to be about the future and now concerned itself solely with the

11

past, for the simple reason that we had already gained the future which we had dreamed of and consequently could no longer recreate the present into a new future in our imagination.

❋   ❋   ❋

Two weeks later I found myself again sitting at the same table, in almost the same company, and occupying the same chair. By this time they had had occasion, each one in his own community, to think over answers to all the enunciations which, out of politeness, they had allowed to remain unanswered. Now they came armed; and this time the re-union turned sour. Those who were tired, lazy, or preferred good food, did not bother to argue, stepped aside, and left silence behind them. But those who were eager for a fray commenced to battle. The secret program, which had never been quite clearly formulated, was changed, and they accused one another of defection.

—"No, I have never been an atheist!" screeched one.

—"Oh? Haven't you?"

And with that a discussion commenced that ought to have taken place twenty years earlier. Everyone tried to do consciously what he had done unconsciously during the happy days of their youth. Their memory of things failed them. They had forgotten what they had done or said then. When they quoted themselves and others, they quoted erroneously. And so a tumult ensued. At the first hint of silence, they repeated what had been said before, and the conversation went like a tread-wheel. After that, silence set in. And then it started all over again.

This time they parted with a feeling that they were through with the past and that they had come of age; that they were entitled to leave the nursery behind and shoot up freely by themselves, transplanted in the open, without gardener, shears and label.

That is mainly how it happened that these people came to be alone; and this is no doubt how it has always been. Yet it was not quite the end. For some of them—who were not eager to have their growth stunted but wished to go ahead, open up new fields, conquer new worlds—stuck together and formed a little group, using the café as a meeting place. Attempts had naturally been made to meet at the homes of the various members of the group, but it soon became apparent that the member-host had inside his coat a lining commonly called wife. And more frequently than not, this caused a strain in the seams. Whenever she was present the conversation had to detour to something else. And if one forgot oneself and began to talk about one's own problems or interests, two things were likely to occur. Either the wife took the speaker's chair and determined all questions dictatorially—and then one had to be polite and say nothing—or she would get up, run out into the nursery, and not become visible again until it was time to sit down and eat. And at table one felt like a beggar and a parasite, and was treated as if one were trying to entice the husband away from house and home, from duty and his plighted troth.

In this manner things could not go on; and it was most frequently through antipathy between the wives that friendships came to an end, for they always found fault with one another.

So the café turned out to be the meeting place, after all. But strangely enough, they did not feel quite so much at home there as before. Unquestionably they tried to convince themselves that this was the neutral place for conviviality because no one was host and no one guest. But the ones who were married and had someone sitting at home by herself felt an anxiety for the little woman. She was doomed to sit at home by herself, while—had she not been married—she could have found someone else to keep her company. And besides, the guests at the café were mostly unmarried; consequently, enemies of a kind. And being, so to speak, without a home of their own, they seemed to have special privileges here. They behaved as if they were at home, made a lot of noise, laughed boisterously, and regarded those who were married as interlopers. In short, they were a disturbing influence.

Being a widower, I felt I had a certain right to come to the café. But I must have been wrong in assuming that. When I persuaded those who had wives to join us there, I soon brought the hatred of their wives down upon me. And so it was not long before I ceased to be invited to these homes. And there may have been a certain justification for this, for marriage is, after all, a union of two.

When the men did come, they were frequently so taken up with their family affairs that I was first subjected to long recitals of their worries and troubles, with servant-girls and children, school attendance and examinations, until I felt myself so completely involved in other people's sickly household affairs that I began to see that I had gained nothing by tearing myself free from my own domestic worries.

When we at long last came close to the particular subject on the agenda and the more important questions to be discussed, it most often happened that they spoke one at a time while someone else, with downcast eyes, waited for a chance to rebut. He waited for an opportunity to talk about his own difficulties; and this turned out to be in no way a rejoinder but mere dull platitudes without either rhyme or reason. Or it could happen that, in completely demoniacal fashion, all spoke at the same time, without anyone of them understanding what the rest were trying to say. A confusion of tongues which ended in quarreling and made it impossible to grasp what anyone had to say.

—"You don't understand a word I am saying!" was the usual cry of distress.

That is the way it proceeded! Each one had in the course of years given new meanings to words, new values to old thoughts —except that they all refused to divulge what they thought deep down in their hearts. This they kept as a professional secret, or as philosophical tenets of an imaginary future, and of these they were jealous.

Each night when I returned home from one of these café meetings, I felt the worthlessness, the emptiness of these dissipations, which in reality were nothing but a means to be heard and to force one's own opinions upon others. My brain was as if lacerated or disjointed, and sown with seeds of some poisonous weed, which had to be raked up before it began to take root. And when I came home to my loneliness, with its silence, I regained my own self, wrapped myself in my own mental and

14

intellectual atmosphere. In this I felt as much at home as one does in a well-fitting garment, and I sank into an annihilating sleep, liberated from desires, yearnings and will-power.

Gradually I stopped going to the café. I practiced the habit of being alone, but fell back into the old temptation. And with each time I withdrew from the group, I was a little more cured —until at last I felt the great satisfaction of hearing the silence and of listening to the new voices that are to be heard in it.

II

In this summer I gradually came to be alone and restricted to the superficial form of intercourse to which I was constrained by my work and which was mostly maintained by telephone. I will not deny that the beginning was hard and that the vacuum in which I was enveloped clamored to be filled. By severing the contact with fellow-humans I seemed at first to lose strength, but simultaneously I began, so to speak, to coagulate, to condense into a core, or kernel. Within this, everything that I had experienced was stored, digested, and absorbed as nutritional substance for my soul. In addition, I became used to transforming everything I heard and saw: in the house, in which I lived, in the street, in nature. And—bringing it all into relationship with the work I was in the throes of doing—I sensed how each chapter grew. And the studies I made in my solitude I found more valuable than those I made of people in social life.

Twice I have had a home of my own, but I now live in two furnished rooms which I rent from a widow. It took me some time before I could identify with this furniture, belonging to a stranger. But I got over it. The writing table was the hardest object to accept and to live with, for I felt that the deceased member of the Magistrate's Court must have spent a life-time sitting there with his documents. He has left marks from his horrible cyan-blue ink, which I detest; his arm has rubbed off the polish on the right; and on the left he has securely glued a round piece of oilcloth with the most frightful grayish-yellow colors, as a place for the lamp. This annoys me indescribably, but I am determined to make the best of it. The bed—alas, it had been my dream to finish my life on bedding of my own— but although I can afford it, I do not wish to start buying anything again; for to own nothing is a part of freedom. To own nothing, to wish for nothing, is to make oneself impervious to the worst blows of fate. But if one at the same time has enough money to acquire whatever one likes to have, that is good fortune. For it means independence—and independence is another aspect of freedom.

On the walls hang a motley collection of bad paintings, and also some lithographs and chromos. I detested them in the beginning as being ugly, but before long I developed an interest in them that I had not at first anticipated. When I once during my writing felt myself bankrupt of ideas and was struggling for a determining scene, I cast an agonizing glance toward the wall. There my eyes fastened onto an appalling reproduction in color, which at one time had been given as a prize or bonus by some illustrated periodical. It represented a peasant standing on a pier and leading a cow. The two were to board a ferry that, however, was not visible. The lone man, drawn with the sky as background—his one and only cow—his tortured look . . . I found my scene. But there were also in these two rooms a great many knick-knacks, such as collect only in a home, and from which emanates the fragrance of memories—things not purchased but made by friendly hands. Antimacassars, slip-covers, what-nots, and shelf-brackets with glassware and porcelain. Among these I notice a large cup with the inscription: "From grateful . . . etc." All these little mementoes radiate friendliness, gratitude, perhaps even love. And before many days have passed, I feel from these rooms that I am welcome here. All this, which once belonged to another, I have now inherited from a man who is dead and whom I never knew. . . .

My landlady, who immediately saw that I was talkative, is possessed of both culture and tactfulness. She always sees to it that my rooms are tidied up in time for my return from my usual morning walk. When we first greeted each other, it was merely with a friendly nod which said all that was needed to be said: "Howdoyoudo?—Very well, thank you!—Are you comfortable here?—Indeed, splendidly!—I am glad to hear it!"

However, after a week had passed, she could not contain herself and was impelled to ask whether there was not anything that I wished for. All I had to do was to speak up.

17

"No, my dear madam, there is nothing I wish for. Everything here suits me."

"H'm. I only thought—I know how particular most gentlemen are."

"I rid myself of that habit long ago!"

The old woman looked at me with curiosity in her eyes as if she had heard a different story about me.

"Well, but how about the meals?"

"The meals? I haven't noticed anything about them—consequently they must be very good."

And the food *was* good! But not only the food. I was in every way more than taken care of. I felt myself nursed, petted—and that was something I had never experienced before.

Life passed quietly, calmly, and with gentle friendliness. And even though I was occasionally tempted to engage in conversation with my landlady, especially when she seemed to be worrying about something, I conquered the temptation. For I feared not only to be drawn into the tangled affairs of others but I also did not wish to intrude upon the private secrets of her life. I wanted our relations to be impersonal, and found it more in keeping with my mood to place her previous life in an acceptable but shadowy light. Were I to learn of her past, the furniture would take on a different character than I had invested it with; and then my image of her would be torn to shreds. Tables, chairs, buffet, china-closet, bed—all would be nothing but properties in her series of dramas; and I would be confronted with the ghosts associated with them. No, what was here was now mine. I had covered them with the slip-cover of my spirit, and the stage setting had to serve in my own drama alone. In mine!

*   *   *

I have now procured for myself an impersonal circle of acquaintances which I have acquired in a very inexpensive way. During my morning walks I have made these unknown acquaintances, with whom I exchange no greetings because I do not know them personally. The first one I meet is the Major. Because he has retired he receives a pension and consequently has had his fifty-fifth birthday. He is in civilian dress. I know what his name is and have heard a few stories about his younger days. I also know that he is a bachelor. He is, as I mentioned, pensioned off, and therefore goes about without anything to do, just waiting for life to desert him. But he faces his future with courage: erect and straight-backed, and with expanded chest, he usually marches along, with coat unbuttoned and dashing in spirit, undaunted and gallant. His hair is dark, and so is his mustache, his walk so buoyant and elastic that I always straighten up when I meet him. And when I consider that he has passed his fifty-fifth year, I feel myself younger. Somehow I have also gotten the impression from an expression in his eyes that he does not dislike me and may even have taken a liking to me. And after a time he strikes me as an old acquaintance to whom I am disposed to nod. But there is a definite distinction between us: he has served out his time in the army, while I am still in the midst of the battle and struggling to go forward. So it is not worth his trouble to look for sympathy as of some fellow delinquent, remiss in his duty. That is something I would strenuously resist. I admit I am graying at the temples, but I know that my hair could be just as dark as his if I so desired. However, I do not care to, for I have no woman to strut and swagger for. Besides, I think his hair is smoothed down much too much not to cause suspicion while my own can not be open to any such doubt.

And then I encounter another person who possesses the delectable charm of being completely unknown to me. He is, I am certain, past sixty, and his hair and full beard are evenly gray. At the beginning of our acquaintance I seemed to recognize certain features in his splenetic physiognomy, certain lines in his figure, and I approached him with a feeling of compassion and sympathy. He appeared to me to have tasted the bitterness of life in its harshest form, to have struggled against the current and been bruised by it. I also felt that the new era which had grown up imperceptibly and in which he now lived, had left him behind. He could not let go of the ideals of his youth because they were precious to him, and he still felt he was travelling the right road. . . . Poor man! He thinks—he is convinced—that his way is the right way and that the present generation has strayed. . . . It is tragic!

But when I looked into his eyes one day, I discovered that he hated me—perhaps because he had read a feeling of sympathy in my own eyes, and that was what wounded him most. Why, he actually sniffed and snorted at me as he passed. Isn't it also possible that I, without being conscious of it, had hurt or offended him, or someone close to him; that I had meddled in his fate with a careless hand—or could I, perhaps, actually have known this man at one time? He hates me and, strangely enough, I feel as if I deserve his hate. But I do not want to look into his eyes again, for they sting me and give me a bad conscience. It could also be possible that we were born to be enemies; that class difference, blood, birth, breeding and outlook on life have set up barriers between us; and that we are unconscious of it. For I have learned through experience to differentiate between friend and foe among those whom I encounter on my walks. Indeed, there are persons, to me unknown, who radiate enmity to such a degree that I cross the street in order not to come near to them. And this sensitivity is heightened to such a measure of perfection that even when I hear a human voice in the street, it either gives me a feeling of exhilaration or produces an emotion of discomfort—or I feel nothing at all.

Then there is a third one. He rides horseback, and I nod to him. I have known him since my university days. His name is more or less familiar to me but I don't know how to spell it. I have not spoken with him for years, only nodded to him in the street. Sometimes he has recognized my greeting with a smile. And he has a pleasant smile, protruding from under his big mustache. He wears a uniform, and with the years the stripes on his cap have increased in number and become wider and wider. When I recently saw him on his horse, after an interval of ten years, he had so many of them that I was reluctant to greet him, for fear that my salutation would not be returned. He must have sensed what was in my mind, for he pulled up his horse and called to me: "Howdoyoudo! Don't you recognize me?"

Yes, I did, and we went on, each one in his own direction. And after that, the noddings continued. One morning I detected a curious, half suspicious curve on his lip under the mustache. I was uncertain as to how to interpret it—or whether to presume to interpret it—that is how preposterous it seemed to me. It looked—this was merely imagination on my part, of course,—it looked to me as if he wondered whether I was arrogant. I? Such an instance is not a rare one: people underestimate themselves, even though they have the reputation of carrying that mortal sin arrogance on the sleeve of their hearts.

*   *   *

And then I meet an elderly woman, who is taken for a walk by her two dogs. When the dogs stop, she stops; and they stop at every lamppost, every tree trunk, every street corner. Whenever I see her, my thoughts go to Swedenborg: I think of the misanthrope who is left so isolated from the world, so alone, that he is obliged to keep company with animals. And in my imagination I placed her in the category of the punished. She believes she is the mistress of these two unclean animals; instead it is they who compel her to give in to their every whim. I have nicknamed her the Queen of the Universe, or the Protectress of the Universe. For that is what she looks like, with the nape of the neck resting on her back and her eyelids turned toward the ground.

Finally there is my tithes-woman, whom I look upon as having a sixth sense. I rarely see her, yet always when I have received a large sum of money or when she is facing any imminent difficulty. I have never put any credence in 'encounters' of that sort, or in superstitions; have never avoided old crones or hags, or spat after a cat; I have never given a friend a kick in the pants when he was about to start a new undertaking with doubtful chances for success. I have merely wished him godspeed from the bottom of my heart, with a pat on the shoulder. I did so not long ago to an intelligent actor. He turned around, his eyes emitting sparks, and hissing with rage. "Don't ever use that word! It means bad luck!"—I answered him: "No! Even if it does not help, a godspeed can never bring ill luck!" He stuck to his notion because he was superstitious, like all those who have no faith. They believe in everything, but in reverse. If they have a pleasant dream during the night it means something unpleasant; if they dream about vermin, for example, it means money. For my own part, I pay no attention to trivial dreams. But if I should have a dream which forces itself upon me quite naturally, then I interpret it straightforwardly, without turning it about. Consequently a horror dream becomes a warning to me, and a beautiful dream an encouragement or a consolation. This is purely logical and scientific; for if I have a clean heart, I see things in a pure light, and if I have not, the other way around. In dreams, my spirit within is mirrored, and thus I can use them in the same way as I use my shaving mirror: by seeing what I am doing I avoid cutting myself. The same is the case with certain 'happenings' during our waking hours—yet not all. I frequently see slips of paper lying in the street. But it is not all paper slips that attract my attention. If anyone should call my attention to such a piece of paper, however, and I find, on looking at it closely, that something is written or printed on it that in some way coincides with what is occupying my mind, I regard it as an expression of my innermost unborn thought. And in that I am no doubt right, for if this bridge of my thought between the spirit and the mundane did not exist, there would be no way of crossing over the bridge. I am not inclined to believe that people go about and place slips of paper for my benefit. But there *are* people who do think so. And such a thought lies close at hand for anyone whose sole faith is in manmade things and works of human hands.

However, I call my old woman occult because I am at a loss to know why she always appears at just the opportune time. She looks like one of those women I used to see selling things in the square when I was younger. Or one of those you saw selling candy at some stand out in the open. Her clothes have an ashen look but are without patches, and are free from spots. She has no idea who I am and calls me 'governor'!

This is probably because I was portly three years ago, and

it was then that our acquaintance began. Her gratitude and well-wishes follow me part of the way, and it is with pleasure I hear the velvety old words "Bless you!" They have such a different sound from those harsh words "Damn you!"—and I feel that they have a beneficial influence upon me all through the day.

When I at the end of our first year of acquaintance gave her a five-crown note, I expected that she would show that same sort of stupid, idiotic, almost mean expression in her face that poor people get when they are given a good deal more than they feel they deserve. They look, namely, as if they thought you were not right in the head or as if you had picked the wrong bill out of your wallet. A gangster boy always runs away laughing when you give him a silver coin. It is as though he were afraid that you would pursue him and want to exchange the silver coin for one of copper. But my old woman grasped me by the hand so firmly that I could not get free; and with a tone of infinite knowledge of human nature she asked, almost affirmatively: "Mr. Governor, you must have been poor yourself once?" —"Yes—as poor as you—and might be so again!"—She understood; and I wondered whether she had known better days. But I never asked her.

These human beings became practically my sole companions out-of-doors, and during the course of three years I followed them with interest.

But I had also started an association in the house where I lived. Living four flights up, I have the fates of four families, including the people on the first floor, placed in layers underneath me. I have no social intercourse with any of them, have no idea what they look like, do not think I have even met them on the stairs. I only see their name-plates; and by the morning newspapers stuck in their letter-boxes I can judge somewhat whose spiritual children they are. In the house next door, wall to wall with me, lives a singer who sings for me very beautifully. And she has a friend who visits her and plays Beethoven for me. They are my favorite neighbors, and there are times when I am tempted to look them up and make their acquaintance so that

I might thank them for all the cheerful moments they have given me. But I conquer the temptation because I suspect that if we should succumb to the use of banal words the most beautiful in our relationship would be lost.

From time to time no sound comes from these friends of mine, and that has an effect on my state of mind. But then I have another neighbor—I think he lives on one of the lower floors in the adjoining house—and he is a cheerful and merry person. He plays pieces that sound as if they came from some operetta with which I am not familiar. And it is all so irresistibly comical and innocently indecent that I am forced to smile, even when occupied in serious thought.

As a counter-balance and shadow, my nearest neighbor on the floor below keeps a dog. It is a huge, reddish, wildly mad hound that scampers up and down the stairs. Its owner seems to look upon the house as his personal property and us others as house-breakers. And in conformity with this view, he allows this paragon of a watchdog to patrol the stairway. If I occasionally am out late at night and grope about and fumble on the dark stairs and suddenly graze against something soft and shaggy—then the silence of the night is at once broken. In the darkness I see two phosphorous pearls flashing savagely, and from top to bottom can be heard a reverberating racket—a racket that is followed by the opening of a door, from which a gentleman emerges. With a furious, withering look he practically exterminates me—I, who am the injured party! To be sure, I do not ask for his forgiveness, even though I always feel as if I were the guilty one. But as the whole of mankind is culpable when daring to oppose dogowners, my feeling of guilt persists.

I have always failed to understand how a human being can show such solicitude and feelings of affection for the soul of an animal when he instead could offer his devotion to fellow human beings. And this especially when an animal is so unclean as the dog is, whose whole existence evolves around committing a nuisance. And my neighbor underneath me has a wife and a grown daughter whose feelings about social intercourse with dogs correspond with his. The family is in the habit of giving dog soirées, and at these—gathered around the dining-room table —they hold conversations with the monster. As the dog has never learned to speak, he gives his answers by howling; and then the family laughs in chorus with exultation and pride.

Sometimes I am awakened in the middle of the night by the dog's barking. I can then imagine how delighted the family must be to know that they possess such a watchful and wide-awake beast, which is also able to scent the garbage collectors' wagon through closed windows and through walls. To think that the canine proprietor's happiness may be begloomed by the fact that some unfortunate people have had their night's sleep disturbed, I know to be without foundation. The sacred and priceless gift of sleep, which by some is so dearly bought, is anything but respected by this family. I ask myself now and then what type of insensitive person it might be who in the silence of the night does not sense that those whom they have awakened lie in their beds cursing them! Do they not realize how the justifiable hatred penetrates to them through floors and roofs and walls and bodes them no good?

I once had the audacity to complain about dogs that barked night after night in a house in which I lived. The landlord parried with his own complaint about the baby cries from my apartment. He compared the unclean, noxious beast with a little infant crying with pain. Ever since that occurrence I have decided to make no more complaints. But in order to effect a reconciliation within myself and acquire peace in my relations with human beings, because of the pain I suffer from hating, I have attempted to explain these inhibitions towards animals. It is because they surpass the corresponding affections for human beings that I have made this attempt—without however, being able to arrive at any clear conclusion. And like everything for which there is no explanation, this has a dismal and grewsome effect on me.—If I were to use Swedenborg's method of philosophizing, I would syllogize as follows: compulsorily induced idea, or mental obsession, as punishment.—Let this suffice for the present. For in that case, they are unfortunates, and as such they deserve compassion.

I have a balcony in my apartment, and from there I have an expansive view over heath and lake and bluish-purple woods in the far distance, out toward the open sea. But when I am lying down on my sofa, I see only the sky and the clouds. Then I feel as if I were in a balloon, high above the earth. But suddenly my ear is being tortured by a variety of disconnected little sounds. My neighbor underneath is telephoning and I hear by his accent that he comes from Västergötland. A sick child is crying in one of the apartments below. And in the street, two men have stopped beneath my balcony. They are conversing. And now I am actually listening, with the poet's right to intrude upon what is being said, out in the open air, at least.

—"Well, you see, it just *could* not break even."

—"Has he closed for good now? . . . Yes—it's what I thought would happen."

I understood immediately that the conversation was about the newly opened grocery store on the first floor, which had now been closed for lack of customers.

"No, there are too many of these stores; and this man started out in the wrong way. The first day he took in thirty öre; the second day a customer came in and looked through the telephone directory; and the third they sold a few stamps! Yes, there are many too many of these stores! Good-bye!"

"Good-bye! Are you on your way to the bank?"

"No, I am going down to Skeppsbron to clear some goods through the customs. . . ."

These were the last words in a tragedy to which I was a witness during the past three months and which took place in my house in the following manner.

To the left of the entrance to my house they began to make alterations for a grocery store. They were painting and gilding, lacquering and varnishing. All the while the young shopkeeper took in the splendor from the sidewalk. He gave the impression of being a good salesman. There was something aggressive and juicy about him, something airy, perhaps. But he looked unafraid and full of hope, especially when he came in company with his fiancée.

26

I saw partitions, shelves, drawers and compartments built against the walls. The counter, with the scales on it, was seen in place, and the telephone was hanging on the wall. I remember the telephone especially because it sounded so plaintive through the wall. But I refused to make a complaint, trying hard to get rid of the habit of complaining. But then they started putting up something inside the store, a *pancoupé* with an arcade. It reminded me of theatre; and it was intended to produce an illusion of something extravagant by means of a false perspective.

And after that, the drawers and compartments were filled with an interminable heap of things with or without well-known brand names. This took a whole month. Meantime the enormous windowpane was decorated in grand colors, and on the third day I could read on it: The Östermalm Grocery Shop.

Then I thought with Sophocles:

> Among gifts of the gods good sense is the highest;
> therefore we must ever be on our guard
> not to vex or offend the gods. We pay for our recklessness
> with stinging wounds, for our deeds of insolence;
> and as we grow older
> we finally learn good common sense.

How lacking in common sense this young man was! The idea of advertising himself as the proprietor of the one and only real grocery store when our district has lost no less than two hundred! This is a jest, a trick—it is trampling on others who shall sting you in the heel. It is arrogance, haughtiness, exaggerated belief in yourself!

Anyhow, the newly married owner opened his shop. The display in the window was magnificent, yet I trembled at the thought of what the future would bring him. I wondered whether he had opened the store with savings, an inheritance, or merely with money borrowed against a promissory note.

The first few days things went as I had heard the unknown gossips under my balcony relate. On the sixth day I stopped in-

27

side to buy some stamps. I observed that the clerk stood in the doorway, leaning against the doorpost. This seemed to me a tactical blunder for, in the first place, a customer should be able to enter a store without any obstruction; and secondly, it advertised the fact that there were no customers within. And furthermore, I realized that the proprietor was absent, either out with his young wife, or away on a pleasure trip.

Very well, I stepped inside and was struck with amazement by the mise-en-scène and the elaborate equipment, which led me to think that the owner had been connected with the theatre.

When the dates that I bought were to be weighed, they were not picked up with bare fingers but with two pieces of thin paper. This was in the great tradition and promised well. The items I purchased were of good quality, and I became a customer.

A few days later the owner had returned and stood behind the counter himself. I realized at once that he was a young man of the modern world, for he made no attempt to enter into conversation with me—that was a bygone custom! But he conversed with his eyes, which bespoke respectfulness, confidence and honesty. Yet he could not refrain from playing comedy. He was summoned to the telephone and begged me a thousand times to pardon him before he went to answer it. But it was his bad luck that I had written comedies and had studied both pantomime, dialogue and repartee. Consequently I saw by his facial expression that there was no exchange of words over the telephone, and I could tell by his replies to a feigned conversation that it was merely play-acting.

"Yes, yes!—Yes, yes!—Yes—yes!—Yes—oh, yes! Right away!" And the receiver was put back.

This was intended to represent a requisition. But there was a lack of shadings and transitions. It was, of course, actually innocent foolishness, but I did not like being the victim of it, nor did I relish being kept waiting. Because of this, I was disposed to be critical and started to eye the labels and, in particular, to read the brand names. Without being a connoisseur of wines, I nevertheless, from long ago, remembered that when the name of Cruse et fils appeared on a bottle, it was pure French wine. Now I suddenly saw the name on a label, and surprised at finding Bordeaux wines in a grocery store, I let myself go and bought a bottle at an astonishingly low price.

On arriving home I made a couple of discoveries which, although they did not make me angry, nevertheless caused me to make no more purchases in that store. The dates, which on previous visits had been excellent, he had now mixed with dried ones that had a woody taste, and the wine had quite possibly been bottled by a Cruse—perhaps Robinson Crusoe!—but it was definitely not Cruse et fils.

After that day I saw no one going into that shop. And here is where the tragedy begins. A man in his best years, filled with a desire to work, yet doomed to idleness, and perhaps subsequently to downfall and destruction. The battle against ruination, which with every moment of the day came closer! His intrepidity was broken down, and in its stead came a nervous defiance and bravado. Through the window I could observe his face as he, ghostlike, looked for a customer. But after a time he went into hiding. It was a horrid spectacle to see him cringing in back of his arcade, afraid of everything and everybody, even startled and timid at the arrival of a customer. He was always fearful that someone would come in merely to look up an address in the city directory. This was the most cruel and trying moment for him because he was obliged to assume a friendly smile and look pleasant. When first he opened the store he had at one time surprised his clerk snappishly tossing the directory on the counter at a distinguished looking elderly gentleman. With his somewhat shrewder knowledge of human nature, he had rebuked the young man, trying to make him understand that the sale of a stamp, or a look in the directory, might be the means of gaining a new customer. However, he himself had not learned the lesson that dependable goods are the best advertisement, and that by employing spurious methods one fools nobody but oneself.

The dissolution was approaching. I suffered through all his

agony, thought about his wife, the impending date for the repayment of loans, including the promissory note, and the rent. Finally I could not bear to pass his window and went roundabout instead. But still I could not get away from him, for his telephone wire gave out such plaintive sounds through the wall, even during the night, and then I heard tragic moanings—long drawnout, breathless outpourings about an existence which at its very beginning had been shattered: about hopes, about the agonizing thought that it would now be impossible for him to start all over again . . . and forever about his wife, who was now expecting her unborn child.

That the fault was his own did not help the matter and, besides, there may be some doubt that the blame was entirely his. All these little tricks which are practiced by tradesmen, he had had drummed into him by those who in the past had employed him; and he could see nothing wrong in them. Imprudence, injudiciousness were at the root of it all. Yes, these were the causes; the culpability was not his.

I sometimes ask myself why I had to feel concern for all this. Perhaps we should detach ourselves from other people's sufferings. But when we try to avoid them by isolating ourselves from them, they thrust themselves upon us.

The storekeeper's fate was completed, however. It was actually a relief to see the doors being closed, closed for good. But when they opened again to remove the equipment and employees began to empty the boxes and drawers, take down the shelves with groceries and cart away all the merchandise, a great deal of which was spoiled, it was like attending an autopsy. Being acquainted with one of the men, I stepped inside and went into the room behind the arcade. Here was where the owner had fought his battle. To pass the time away and to escape the cursed plight of complete inactivity, he had scribbled imaginary bills in great numbers. They still lay about, and they were made out to Prince Hohenloe, President Félix Faure of France, and one of them even to the Prince of Wales. The latter had "purchased" two hundred kilo of Marmalade Russe and a case of curry.

To me it was interesting to see how the man's brain had jumbled together Félix Faure's Russian Journey and the Prince of Wales' British-Indian cuisine.

There also lay a batch of advertisements, written by hand, itemizing select caviar, top brand coffee,—everything was first class quality—but the advertisements never saw print.

I now understood why he had felt impelled to play this farcical game at his desk. It was done to dupe his clerk. Poor man! But life has a way of going on and is full of changes; and that man, I have no doubt, will extricate himself and come up in the world again.

✿   ✿   ✿

III

This is the ultimate in solace: to spin oneself into the silken threads of one's own soul, to be transformed into a chrysalis and then wait for the metamorphosis—for that is bound to take place. In the meantime one exists with the help of past experiences and lives the lives of others telepathically. Death and resurrection—a new education for something new and unknown to come.

Eventually one is the sole master of one's own being. In my own case, no one else's thoughts control mine, no one's tastes or whims can constrain me or bring pressure to bear upon me. Now my soul is beginning to grow in newly gained freedom, and I experience an indescribable inner peace and a quiet feeling of security and self-responsibility.

When I think back upon my married life—a union that should be an education—I come to the conclusion that it was nothing but a co-educational institution for vice. To be forced continually to see what is unbeautiful is torture for anyone who possesses a sense of beauty, and tends to delude one into thinking oneself being martyred. To shut one's eyes to what is wrongful and evil out of consideration for others breeds hypocrisy. For the self-same reason, to acquire the habit of continually suppressing one's opinions makes one a coward. And finally, to take the guilt upon oneself for something of which one is not guilty, merely for the sake of keeping the peace, debases one unconsciously, so that one fine day one imagines oneself to be a wretch. Never to be given a word of encouragement robs one of fortitude and self-assurance; and to have to bear the consequence of other people's mistakes and errors creates feelings of outrage and vindictiveness against humanity and the order of things. And the worst of it is that we—even with the best of will to do what is right—are without control over our own fate. Of what avail is it to seek to do the right thing if my partner in life disgraces herself? More than half of the shame, if not the whole of it, will redound upon me. This is what usually happens. That is what makes marital partnership so insecure; it offers a wider target for blame when one is personified through another and is at the mercy of another's capricious, arbitrary behavior. And those who were unable to poke their hand inside my waistcoat when I stood alone, can so easily find an opportunity to plunge a knife in my heart if I let another wear it about on the streets and in the market-places.

Still another thing that I have gained by being alone is the freedom to decide for myself about my spiritual diet. I no longer am under obligation to have enemies seated at table with me and to be forced to listen to things which I hold sacred, being reviled and blasphemed, without my being allowed to say a word. I am no longer forced to listen to music of the sort that I abhor, being played in my rooms. I do not have to see newspapers with caricatures of my friends and myself lying about. I am saved from reading books that I disdain and from going to exhibitions to admire paintings by people for whom I have no regard. In short, I am master of my soul, at least in those circumstances in which I have a right to make a decision. And I am free to make my own choice when it comes to antipathies and sympathies. I have never been a tyrant; I have simply refused to be tyrannized. And that is something which the tyrannical person can not forgive.

I have always wished to go forward and upward, and therefore have had the more eminent right on my side against those who have tried to pull me downward; that is the reason for my being alone, for staying away from people.

✻ ✻ ✻

The first thing one is faced with in solitude is the settlement with oneself and the past. This is a long drawn-out task and a consummate education in the conquest of oneself. But if it is possible to learn to know oneself, it is, indeed, a most grateful study. One is, to be sure, obliged to use a mirror from time to time, especially a handmirror, since it would otherwise be difficult to know how one looks from the back.

The reconciliation I prepared for, began ten years ago, after I had become acquainted with Balzac. While perusing his fifty volumes, I was unaware of what took place within me until the reconciliation was complete. Then I had found myself and was able to resolve the synthesis of all the opposing words, ideas, and actions throughout my life which had hitherto remained unsolved. But by looking at human beings through Balzac's perspective lenses, I also learned to view life with both eyes, while previously I had looked at it through a monocle and with one eye. And he, the great magician, had filled me not alone with a certain resignation, a submissiveness to fate or Providence, which spared me the pain of feeling the worst blows, but had as well —without my being conscious of it—infused in me a species of religious faith, which I should like to call non-denominational Christianity. During my pilgrimage through his The Human Comedy, guided by Balzac's hand, I there made the acquaintance of four thousand human beings (a German has counted them!). And I felt myself living another life, broader and richer than my own, so that when I had finished the book, it seemed to me that I had lived two separate lives. Through his world I gained a fresh viewpoint of my own life; and after relapses and crises I at last arrived at a kind of reconciliation to suffering. Simultaneously I discovered how the refuse of the soul was, so to speak, burned away by sorrow and suffering, refining the instincts and feelings and endowing me as well with superior capabilities after my soul had been liberated from my tortured body. From then on I took the bitter cups of life as medicine and considered it my duty to suffer whatever life sent me—all except debasement and bondage.

But being alone tends to make one sensitive and irritable, and while I formerly had armed myself against suffering by being inhuman and ruthless, I now grew to be more sensitive to the sufferings of others; indeed, became victim of external influences, although not of sinister influences. These only fright-

34

ened me and made me withdraw even further into my cocoon. They forced me to seek a more secluded path for my walks, where I would only encounter people of a class that did not know me. I have a special such pathway, to which I refer as Via Dolorosa. I take this path when I feel more depressed than usual. It is near the limits of the city's boundary line to the north, an avenue with a row of houses on one side and woods on the other. But in order to reach it, I must take a narrow cross-street which has a special attraction for me without my being conscious of the reason for it. This narrow street is dominated at its terminal point by a large church which casts a shadow, while at the same time it exalts. It does not tempt me, however, because—well, I don't know why. Down below is the parish-registrar's office where I long ago asked to have the banns published. But way up here to the north stands a house, precisely where the street emerges into the heath.

It is big as a castle, stands on the extreme mountain slope and faces the inlet of the sea. For several years my thoughts have been occupied with this house. I have had a desire to live there; I have imagined that someone lives there who has had an influence upon my destiny, or who still has. I can see the house from where I live, and I gaze at it whenever the sun illuminates it, or when it is lighted up at night. And when I pass by it, a friendliness and sympathetic affinity seems to emanate from it and makes me feel as if I would like to dwell in it some day and there find peace.

And so I stroll along the avenue, where a great many cross-streets terminate; and every one of them brings back some memory from my past. Because I am standing on a hillside, the streets slope downward, but some of them take first a winding turn and form a low elevation that has the shape of an earth globe. Standing on the sidewalk of the avenue and seeing a person coming from behind this elevation, you notice first a head sticking up from the ground, then the shoulders, and finally the rest of the body. This happens within thirty seconds and has a most mysterious effect.

As I pass, I look down into every cross-street and they all show in the distance either the southern part of the city, the royal palace, or the city between the bridges. And all the while I am assailed by memories from each district. Down there at the bottom of that crooked, curving thoroughfare which is called ***** Street stands a house where I went in and out a generation ago while my fate was spinning its net. . . . Directly opposite stands another house where twenty years later I passed my days under similar conditions, yet in reverse, and then doubly painfully. Down on the next street I lived through days which in the life of others usually are the most beautiful. They are so to me also, yet at the same time the ugliest. And the varnish of time could not bring out the beautiful; it coated it over with the ugly. A painting has a habit of flattening with the years, and the colors change, yet not to their advantage; for the white, in particular, has a tendency to turn a dirty yellow. Pietists say that this is as it should be in order that we, when arriving at the parting-way of life, may joyfully turn our backs upon all that is mundane.

As I proceed up the avenue, past the newly built big houses, these gradually begin to thin out. The knobs of rock come into view, a tobacco-growing tract stretches across a field; a local butcher has his ramshackle hovels cut off by the bend of an alley. There I see a tobacco barn which I recall from—1859. I used to play inside it. In a little house, which now is no more, lived a charwoman who at one time was nursemaid in my parents' home . . . and from the roof of that barn her eight-year-old son fell to the ground and hurt himself badly. We used to come here to ask her to help us with the big house-cleaning at Easter and at Christmas time . . . and I liked to take these backstreets on my way to school and thus avoid Drottninggatan. Here I could see trees and blooming plants; cattle grazed here and hens cackled—such was the landscape in those days! . . .

And now I sank back in time to my dismal childhood when the unfathomable that life had in store for me, lay frighteningly before me. Everything weighed down upon me and oppressed me. . . . I need only turn on my heels to put it behind me, and I do so—yet I cast a fleeting glance at the tops of the linden trees in the long street of my childhood and at the shadowy contours of the pine trees out by the city's compound for vehicles.

I have turned my back on all this and now when I look down the avenue, with the sun in the distance, across bluish rock formations at the shore, I forget for a moment all this about my childhood, which is so entangled with the fate of others and therefore is not my own life. For my own life begins out there by the sea. . . .

That corner over by the tobacco barn is my particular dread. Still it attracts me now and then with the same fascination as all that is painful does. It is much like going to see safely chained wild beasts that cannot attack you. And the momentary pleasure I experience when I turn my back on it all, is so intense that I occasionally gratify it. In that moment I cover thirty-three years of time, and it gladdens me to be standing where I stand. Besides, as a child I always had a yearning "to be old," and I believe now that I had a premonition of what was in store for me. Even now I believe my life experience was pre-determined and therefore inescapable. When I encountered Minerva and Venus at the cross-roads of youth, it was of no use to make a choice. So I followed both, hand in hand,—as no doubt all of us have done, and as, perhaps, we all should do.

However, as I now walk with the sun in my face, I come before long to a wood of spruce on my left. There, I recall, I used to take walks twenty years ago, observing the city below me. I was then an outcast, an outlaw, because I—like Alcibiades—had profaned the mysteries, and because I had overthrown the images of the gods. I remember how dismal I felt, for I knew I did not have a solitary friend; and down there below the entire city held forth like an army against me alone. I saw the watch-fires, heard the alarm-bells and knew that they would capture me through starvation. I now know that I was in the right; but that I took malicious joy in the conflagration I had started—that was my error. If I had only had a spark of compassion for the feelings

37

of those whom I had wounded! If . . . ! But I presume that would have been asking too much of a young man who had never received any sympathy from those others!

My walks through the woods are brought back to me as something rich and solemn. That I did not succumb then, I do not ascribe to my own strength, for in that I have no faith.

*   *   *

For the last three weeks I had not spoken with any human being, and as a result my voice had, so to speak, been locked in, had lost its ring and become muffled. When I spoke to the maid, she did not understand what I said and I was obliged to repeat my words several times. Then I grew anxious, felt my solitude as banishment, and the thought struck me that people refused to have anything to do with me because I had rejected them.

And so I went out in the evening. I took a seat in a streetcar, merely to get the feeling of being close to others. I tried to read in their glances whether they hated me, but I read only indifference. I listened to their conversation as if I had been at a social gathering and were entitled to take part in the conversation, at least as a listener. When the car grew crowded, it gave me a strange sense of satisfaction to feel myself rubbing elbows with other human beings.

I have never hated people, rather the opposite, but I have always been in fear of them, ever since I was born. My inclination to be sociable and convivial has been so pregnant that I have been able to be companiable with anyone; and in the past I have looked upon solitude as a punishment—which it may well be. I have asked friends who have been in prison, wherein their punishment principally consisted, and their answer has been: the solitude.

This time, it is true, I have sought to be alone, but I made a mental reservation that I should allow myself to look up my acquaintances whenever I felt an urge to do so. Why don't I do it? I cannot, for—as I climb the stairs—I feel like a beggar, and turn about without ringing the doorbell. And when I am back home again, I feel undisturbed in mind, especially when

I recapitulate in my imagination what I think I would have heard if I had rung the bell and entered. Since my thoughts do not team with anyone else's, I am wounded by almost everything that is being said. Even an innocent word I often feel to be a taunt, a derision.

I think it must be my destiny to walk alone, and that this is best for me. I like to believe it to be so, else it would all be too irreconcilable. But in solitude the mind becomes at times overloaded and threatens to explode. Thus one must watch oneself. I try constantly to keep the balance between the outgoing and the incoming. Every day I must have an outlet through my writing; and through reading I receive fresh impulses and inspiration. If I write the whole day, it brings an agonizing emptiness in the evening. I get the impression that I have nothing more to say, and that I have come to the end. If I read the whole day I am glutted, surfeited, and I feel as if I were about to burst. I must, furthermore, choose the time for sleeping and for waking. Too much sleep tires and turns into torture; too little sleep sets one's nerves on edge and can produce hysteria.

The day passes easily enough, but the evening is trying, for to feel one's intelligence dulled or benumbed is as painful as to feel oneself deteriorating spiritually and physically.

When I, after a sober evening and restful sleep, get up in the morning, life is a veritable joy. It is like rising from the dead. All the capacities of the soul have been regenerated, and the strength fused together by sleep seems to be doubled many times over. Then I feel as if I had the capacity to alter the order of the universe, rule the fate of nations, declare war and topple dynasties. When I read the newspaper and through the foreign dispatches see the changes being wrought in current world history, I get a feeling that I am a part of the times, in the very midst of the events of our era as they unfold at this very moment. I am "a contemporary," and I sense it as if I in some small measure have been instrumental in shaping this new age through my contribution in the past. After that, I read about my country, and end by reading about the city where I was born.

Out of the yesterdays the history of the world has advanced.

Laws have changed, trade routes have been opened, the order of succession to thrones has been dislocated, constitutions of nations have been regenerated. Human beings have died, others have come into the world, and still others have entered into matrimony.

Since yesterday, the world has changed, and with a new sun and a new day events and happenings have taken place, and I myself feel renewed.

I am burning with desire to start to work, but first I must go out of doors. As soon as I come down to the entrance door, I know at once which way to take. Not alone the sun, the sky, and the temperature give me the direction, but my mood, in which I have a barometer that will tell me how I stand with the world.

I have three roads to choose from. The bright roadway out toward Djurgarden, Strandvägen with its throngs of people, and the other streets, and the lonely Via Dolorosa, which I just mentioned. I know immediately where I am destined to go. If I feel harmonious inside, I am warmed by the gentle air and I seek the presence of human beings.

Then I walk through the streets past the swarming crowds and experience the feeling that they are all friendly toward me. But if anything is awry, then I see only enemies with scornful glances, and sometimes their hate is so strong that I have to turn back. Should I then choose the vicinity near Brunnsviken and the oak hills around Rosendahl, it is possible that nature will smile upon me, and then I am at home as in my own skin.

These surroundings I have screened off, become attached to, and made into a background for my person. But they have a temperament of their own, as well, as there are mornings when we do not get along. At such times everything is different: the triumphal arches of the birches have turned into mere twigs and brushwood; the bewitching arbors of hazel shrubs no longer conceal the distinctive hazel sticks; the oak stretches its craggy arms threateningly over my head, and I feel as if I had hames or a yoke round my neck. This disparity between myself and my landscape strains my nerves to such a degree that I am about to go to pieces and flee. As I then turn and see the southern part of the city and the magnificent contours of the entire capital, I sense it as if I were in the unknown land of an enemy, myself a tourist seeing this for the first time, and feel forsaken like the stranger who knows no one within those walls.

When I, however, have arrived home and am sitting at my writing-table, then I live again; and the energy I have gathered out in the open, whether from the current transformer of disharmonies or the current closer of harmonies, now serves me for my various purposes. I am living, and I live over and over again the human lives I depict; I am happy with those who are happy, irate with those who are irate, and those who are good make me feel good. I creep out of my own personality and speak out of the mouths of children—of women—of old men; I am king and I am beggar; I am the highly placed one, the tyrant, and the most despised among men, the oppressed hater of tyrants; I have a multitude of opinions, and confess to all religions; I dwell in all ages and have ceased to exist as myself. And all this is a state of mind which gives me an indescribable joy. But when this comes to an end around dinner time and I have finished my writing for the day, my own existence becomes so painful that increasingly throughout the evening I feel as if I were about to die. And the evening is horribly tedious and long. Other people generally find diversion in conversation at the end of the day, but I come by none. Finally silence settles around me. I try to read, but I cannot gather my thoughts. I start pacing the floor and watch the clock to see how near it is to ten. And after long waiting, it finally strikes ten.

When I then liberate my body from its clothing with all those hooks, buttons, laces and clasps, my soul, so to speak, seems to catch its breath, and I feel freer. And, following my Oriental ablutions, I go to bed. Then the whole of existence stretches before me. The will to live, the strife, the struggle ceases; and the longing for sleep takes on much the same semblance as the longing for death.

First, however, I meditate for half an hour. What I mean is that I read from a devotional manual which I choose accord-

41

ing to my need. Sometimes I use a Catholic one; it brings with it a breath of the apostolic, traditional Christianity. It is like Latin and Greek—it is history; for in Catholic Christianity our own, *my* culture, has its beginning. With Roman Catholicism I feel myself a Roman citizen, a citizen of Europe. And the interspersed Latin verses are a reminder to me that I am a person of culture. I am not a Catholic, have never been one, for I cannot let myself be bound by any particular confession. That is why I occasionally take an old Lutheran book that has a special text for each day of the year. I use it as a scourge. It was written in the seventeenth century, when mankind had a hard time of it on this earth. Consequently it is terribly severe, preaching suffering as a gift of grace and a blessing. Rarely has the author a good word to say. He could bring you agony, and that is why I struggle against him. "It is not so," I say to myself; it is only a book to test one's strength. Catholicism has taught me, namely, that the Devil—whenever he wishes to cause anyone agony and rob him of hope—appears in his ugliest rôle. But hope is one of the Catholic's virtues, for to believe God to be goodness is the essence of religion. To believe evil of God is satanism.

Occasionally I take a curious book from the period of enlightenment during the eighteenth century. It is written anonymously, and I am at a loss to know whether to ascribe it to a Catholic, Lutheran or a Calvinist. It contains Christian wisdom of life by a man who has had worldly experience and known life and who, as well, is a learned man and a poet. He frequently gives me the answers to just what I need to know for that day and moment. And no sooner have I momentarily reacted severely against his unjust and unreasonable demands of us mortals than he in the next instance parries with my very own objections. He is what I would call a reasonable man who observes with both eyes and who apportions right and wrong, each to its own fold. The author reminds me in some ways of Jakob Böhme, who concluded that to every question there is a 'yes' and a 'no' answer.

At momentous times I must fall back on the Bible. I own several Bibles of various ages, and it appears to me as if in each the contents differed. It is as if they possessed a different intensity of current, a different capacity for making an impression on me. One of my Bibles, bound in black cordovan leather, printed in Schwabach in the seventeenth century, exudes an enormous potency. It once belonged to a family of clergymen, whose ancestry is written down on the insides of the covers. It is as though hatred and anger had accumulated in this book. It does nothing but curse and punish. No matter which leaf I turn to, I always come across David's or Jeremiah's damnation of their enemies. But I refuse to read it as it seems to me un-Christian. For example, when Jeremiah prays: "Then punish now their children with starvation and let them perish by the sword so that the wives and widows may be without children, and their husbands slain," etc. These are not the words for a Christian. I can well understand that one prays to God for protection against enemies who are bent upon pulling one down when one is striving upward, against enemies who from evilness take the bread out of one's mouth. I can also understand that one should thank God when one's enemy has been beaten. For all nations have sung a Te Deum after having won a victory. But to pray that specific punishments be meted out to an adversary—that is something I would not dare to do. And I think I can say that what may have seemed fitting for David and Jeremiah in their day, does not seem so to me in my day.—But then I have another Bible, bound in calf skin with gilt lettering, from the eighteenth century. The general contents are, of course, the same as in the Bible just mentioned, but they are presented in a different manner. This book resembles a novel and emphasizes the brighter side. Even the paper is brighter, the typography is clear and luminous, and there is in evidence a desire to speak out and yet be amenable, as Jehovah is to Moses when the latter has the temerity to come with remonstrances which are rather sullen.

For example: when the people have grumbled anew and Moses is sick and tired of it all, he turns to the Lord, almost with reproof: "Have I now begot all these that you should say to me: 'Carry them in your arms as a wet nurse carries an infant. . . .' —Where am I to take meat from to give to all these . . . ? I am not able alone to give sustenance to all these—it is too much of a hardship for me. And if you do this to me, then take my life instead. . . ."

Jehovah's answer to Moses' complaint is not at all unfriendly, and to help him He proposes that he select the seventy elders. This is certainly not the inexorable, revengeful God of the Old Testament. And I do not brood over it. I only know that there are moments when the Old Testament is closer to me than the new one. And there is no doubt that the Bible, for us who are born into Christianity, is an instructive and moral force. Whether our forebears, because of this, ascribed to it psychic powers and at the same time derived such powers from it, is hard to say. Sanctuaries, sacred edifices, and sacred books possess indeed power as accumulators, but solely for those who believe; for faith is my personal battery, and without it I cannot make the silent page speak. Faith is my personal counter-current that produces energy through impulses; faith is the rasper that electrifies the glass slab; faith is the receiver, and must also act as conductor, else there will be no reception; faith is the relinquishing of opposition by the medium through which contact is made.

For this reason all sacred books remain silent to the unbelieving. For the one who does not believe is sterile, his spirit so pasteurized that nothing will take root in it. He is a negation, a minus, an illusive quantity, the wrong side of the coin, the saprophyte who can only exist by living off the roots of something growing. He has no life of his own, since he—in order to negate—must have the positive to negate against.

Finally, there are moments when only some words from Buddha are of help. It is actually so seldom that we get what we wish for. What good, then, is it to ask? Ask for nothing, expect nothing of your fellowmen or of life, then you will have the feeling that you have been given more than what you might have asked for. And you know from experience that when you have received what you yearned for, it was less the gift than the fulfillment itself that gave you joy.

I sometimes ask a spirit within me: "Do you really believe this?" I quickly stifle that voice, for I know that faith is purely a state of soul and not an act of mental reasoning. And I know also that such a state is a healthful one for me and helps to broaden my knowledge.

It happens now and then that I rise up against the unreasonable demands, the extreme, rigid exactions, the inhuman punishments, and then I leave my devotional books for a while. But before long I go back to them, urged by a voice crying in the wilderness from time immemorial: "Remember that you were once a slave in Egypt and were freed by the Lord your God." Then my misgivings are silenced. And I would feel that I was an ungrateful, cowardly wretch if I were to deny my Saviour before mankind.

❁　　　❁　　　❁

IV

It is spring again—for the . . . time. (One does not like to mention years after having reached a certain age.) But spring sets in differently now from what it did years ago. In olden days the transformation began when the ice upon the streets was hacked away about Eastertide. Then one saw the layers that had been formed throughout the winter lying in geological formation with all its many strata. Nowadays such ice deposits are forbidden by law. Sleighs and sleighbells and sleighnets are rarely seen, so that one gets the impression that the climate has changed to resemble that of continental Europe, just as the time has. Previously, when navigation came to a standstill in the autumn and there were no railroads, one was practically isolated. One had to provide for the winter with salted victuals, and when spring set in again, one was awakened to a new life. Now icebreakers and railroads compensate for the unseasonal differences, and flowers, fruits and vegetables can be obtained throughout the year.

In former days the storm-windows had to be removed, and with that the clatter and noise from the street immediately penetrated into the rooms. It was as if one had resumed contact with the outer world. The dull, even, indoor quiet had come to an end, and one was awakened to new life, not least because of the bright daylight which now poured in. Nowadays the storm-windows are left in throughout the whole year, but in compensation the windows that are not taped in can be opened whenever there is need for it.

With such equalizing factors, spring glides in upon us without the trappings of the past. It is therefore welcomed without any particular enthusiasm.

I greeted this year's spring in a matter of fact way and without any great hopes.—It is spring—consequently it will soon be autumn again!—I seated myself on my balcony and gazed at the clouds. By these it can be seen that it is spring. They gather in larger formations, they are denser, their contours more distinct; and when the sky can be discerned through an opening or a rift, it is almost bluish black. But in the distance I see the edge of a wood. It is mostly spruce and fir, greenish black, and jagged, and is to me the most unique part of the Swedish nature. And I point to it and say: This is Sweden!—There are times when the forest skirt takes on the appearance of a city with endless rows of chimneys, church spires, battlements and pinnacles, little towers and gables. But today I see it as a wood. Because a wind is blowing, I take it for granted that the mass of slender trees must be stirring. But I cannot notice any motion, being half a mile from them. Therefore I resort to my binoculars, and now I can see the entire contour of spruce moving like waves against a horizon of sea. This provides me with great pleasure, especially since it appears to be a minor discovery as well. I think there is where my longing goes, for I know that beyond lies the sea; I know that blue anemones and white ones grow at the foot of the trees—yet I take greater delight in seeing them in my imagination than in reality. For I have long ago grown away from those forms of nature that are found in the mineral, the vegetable and the animal kingdoms. It is human nature that interests me, and the fate of mankind.

In the past I could be lost in the sight of a blossoming garden; today I still enjoy the sight of it but not as much as formerly. And I am trying to explain this by the fact that I now divine that there must exist more perfect prototypes of these imperfect images. That is why I have no longing for the country, even though I feel that a faint distaste for the city is beginning to reveal itself. This, however, I sense to be more a sign of the need for change.

And so I walk along on my usual paths; and when I gaze at people's faces, memories rise to the surface and they bring to life thoughts. And whenever I pass shopwindows, I see so many things from every land of the globe which have been made or refined by human hands and they, so to speak, put me in touch with the whole of the universe and provide me with a host of impressions, such as color, shape, and related ideas.

Each morning, when the rooms on the first floor are being dusted and tidied up, one of the windows stands open. I pass it without stopping, of course, yet by a momentary glance I have obtained a view of a room that was unknown to me, and through it a flash of human history. This morning, for instance, I happened to cast a glance through a window with a sliding pane, in an old house, and on the window sill stood an aspidistra. I looked inside between the leaves of this ugly species of the lily family from Japan—which does not bring forth its flower by sunlight but forms it directly from the root down by the soil, with a shape as of small pieces of meat, patterned into stars. And within I saw a writing table with useful and prosaic accessories and beyond it, in a corner, stood a quadrangular porcelain stove of white tile. This stove was of ancient vintage, each tile surrounded with a black mourning border, much like dirt under the nails. It had big doors in front of the grate; and the corner, in which it was placed, was darkened by the indescribably murky wallpaper. At first the room gave me an impression of the 1870's because of its gloominess, but it also communicated to me the abstract unhappiness of a somewhat less than well-off lower middle-class home—of people who had to strain and strive to make ends meet, and who tormented themselves and one another. And this glimpse inside brought back the memory of an old home—a home I should not have thought of had not this sliding window stood open. With this, I envisioned also a long forgotten fate, and I now saw it in a fresh and interesting light; only at this moment did I begin to understand these people as I countenanced them in my thoughts, so many years afterward. I now understand their tragic drama, which I had previously tried to keep away from because it affected me as being petty and painful. When I came home, I outlined the drama. And it had been inspired by a glimpse through an open window!

When I go out of an evening after dark and the houses are lighted up, my knowledge grows richer through familiarity with people, for then I can see into the upper stories also. I there observe furnishings, fixtures and interiors, obtain views of family life, scenes of actual living. People who do not pull down their shades are especially disposed to showing themselves. Therefore I do not need to worry about being indelicate. Besides, I merely take snapshots, later working over what I have witnessed.

One evening, for instance, I passed an attractive corner apartment with large windows, and saw. . . . I saw furniture and other furnishings from the 1860's, together with curtains from 1870, draperies from 1880, and little what-nots with figurines from 1890. In the window was placed an urn of alabaster, yellowed by people's breaths, sighs, tobacco smoke and fumes of wine—an urn without any particular purpose, which someone had eventually destined to serve as a receptacle for visiting cards. An urn for ashes to be placed in a burial mound, inscribed with the names of friends who had lived and died, of relatives who had lived and died, of persons married and engaged, baptized and buried.

On the walls were numerous portraits from all ages and from every century, heroic figures in coats of mail, intellectuals in perukes, clerical men with clergymen's bands. In a corner in front of a divan stood a card table, and seated around it sat four curious characters playing cards. They said nothing, their lips did not move. Three of them were ancient, but one of the men was of middle age and seemingly the head of the house. In the center of the room sat a young woman. She had her back turned to the players and was leaning over her knitting. Even though she was working at something, she performed the task without taking any interest in it. She seemed to be doing it simply to while the time away, measuring the seconds with the needle, stitch for stitch. She held up the knitting and regarded it as if she were reading the time by a watch. But she was looking beyond time and work and into the future. Then her glances leapt through the window, past the urn for ashes, and her eyes met mine out there in the darkness, but without seeing me. I felt as if I knew her, as if she spoke to me with her eyes, but she did not, of course. One of

49

the mummies at the card table said something just then. The young woman answered with a movement of the neck and without turning around. She acted as if she had been disturbed in her thoughts, or perhaps even had had them unmasked, and she bent her head still further down over her knitting and continued measuring the time with her second hand, the needle. Never have I seen the boredom, the weariness, the ennui with life so minutely concentrated as in this room.

The man at the card table, whose face changed expression continually, appeared to be uneasy about something, to be waiting for something, and the mummies reflected the same kind of disquiet and anxiety. Ever so often they would cast a glance toward the wall-clock, whose big hand was approaching the end of an hour. They are no doubt expecting someone—someone who would drive away their weariness and boredom, who would change their fates and bring something new and fresh to them. Perhaps even turn their present existence about completely. Being, as it were, in suspense over this fear, none of them were able to concentrate on the game. They played their cards at random, as if they expected to be interrupted at any moment; nobody waited for either facial expression or gesture. And as a result, their movements seemed much like the movements of mannikins.

Well, what was to happen, did happen.—"What luck!" I thought, when the draperies suddenly moved and a maid in a white cap came in and announced someone. A spark of life flew into all in the room, and the young woman turned half around and got up. Simultaneously the clock on the wall struck so loudly that I could hear it out on the street, and I saw how the minute hand bounded forward toward the full hour.

Just then a passer-by gave me a push which woke me up with such a start that I literally felt myself thrown out on the street from this room, where I had been with my soul for these two long minutes and had lived through a fraction of these persons' existence. Ashamed I continued on my way. My first impulse was to turn back in order to learn what followed, but I changed my mind as this thought came to me: I know the ending in advance, because I myself have experienced similar happenings so many times in the past, over and over again. . . .

Spring is approaching in much the same way as in so many previous years, yet not exactly the same way. In years past, the first sign came from the skylark in the field facing my windows. But now there are no more larks being seen there, and so it is the chaffinch in Humlegarden and the starlings on Fagelbacken that announced the coming of spring. What is unchanged, however, is the moving time in April. To see furniture and household goods and utensils on the sidewalks is a sight that to me has always seemed horrible. These are the belongings of human beings who, without house or home, are forced to show their intestines, and who blush for the ignominy. That is one reason the owner is never seen nearby, watching over his belongings. He prefers to have some stranger look after his things, which advertise their defects in the light of day. The sofa with a table in front of it could pass muster at home, in feeble light, but in stark sunshine the spots and tears and smudges are visible. That the fourth leg is loose mattered little at home, but out here it has fallen off.

If one should see a face behind a cartload of furniture about to be moved, it is a troubled face, full of worry and agony. But I presume that moving and travelling are a part of life. We have to be wrenched, shaken up, renewed, turned inside out. I, who have never done anything but move and travel, am now—while enjoying a life of quiet—given back my impressions from my peripatetic years, and I have condensed them into a poem which I gave the title *Ahasuerus*.

AHASUERUS*

Ahasuerus, out and wander,
Take your knapsack and your staff!
Your fate differs from those yonder—

---

* The poetic parts are freely translated. A.P.

no peace waits for you, nor epitaph.
Cradle had you, life beginning,
but there'll be no end to yours;
and forever, for your sinning,
doomed to suffer from remorse. . . .
While awaiting your Messiah
time has fled and passed you by.
Do you think you'll be delivered?
Do you think you'll be forgiven?
Will you, as was once Elijah,
be redeemed while 'mongst the living?
Out on roads and paths and highways,
far from warmth of hearth and home;
if your fields should be laid waste,
then your house and home are ruined,
like Capernaum in the past;
lost to you are wife and children,
nothing saved, destroyed by flames
land and fields are scorched throughout.

❖   ❖   ❖

Jump on the train with knapsack and staff
and do not look back even once.
Bless Him who took but who also bestowed
and taught you how to forsake.
No kith and kin will stand there and wave
a Godspeed upon your long journey!
No matter! It's easier then
to leap out and weather the cold, cold world!

❖   ❖   ❖

The train gives a start, pulls off from its shed,
a rolling serpent of wooden houses,
a travelling village of men and beasts. . . .
It has cars for mail and freight and restaurants
and has sleeping quarters with heavy curtains.
It now jerks forward irresistibly;

a city on wheels, it travels through walls,
it slithers through mountains like a snake through a shed,
it rolls over water, its fire-horse neighing,
it speeds through a province with seven-league stride;
a shortcut—and soon a kingdom is passed! . . .
The end of the mainland! And now at the sea!
Ahasuerus, now you are free from the land,
and all that formerly bound you to life
is now buried deep, beyond the horizon.

*   *   *

How heavy the clouds are rolling by
and how billowing are the waves!
They rise and they fall, rise and fall,
but they offer for man no foothold,
and for you neither rest nor peace any more!
Neither day nor night, waking or sleeping. . . .
Heaved up and down, pitched hither and thither,
with soughing and creaking in rigging and mast,
and screeching aloft from bolts and rivets.
Torture for body, torture for soul,
a torture rack floating upon the water. . . .
Confess your guilt and think of your soul
whenever you hear the roaring breakers!
You are then not far from the rescuing shore;
but the skipper knows better, sails straight
out to sea, to the open sea he flees—
away from the hoped-for saving port—
and turns his back on the peaceful islands;
for false is the sea, but still falser the coast!
When you sail before the wind with all sails flying,
that's when you can look for the roughest battle. . . .

Out to sea! Set out for the green-gray field out there
where the ship is plowing and the rain clouds sow,
but where nothing grows in the wake of the plow
and nobody lives 'neath the heavenly tent.

This day it looks like a tarpaulin spread
to protect 'gainst the rain that keeps increasing.
To some it may seem as meant for protection
for the firmament's blue 'gainst the steamships' smoke,
the dust from the earth and the specks of the flies,
or to screen out the eyes of the wicked.

✧   ✧   ✧

Ahasuerus stands up forward,
looking toward the wall of gray,
hand is clenched, his eye is tearing,
lips are keen-edged, beard is white.—
Now he has no more illusions,
memories have faded out,
hope itself declines to serve him;
in the present he must live—
and this present is so painful,
has no meaning, has no aim,
mute as answer to a stupid question,
dead as flint without the steel.
Staring into space the wand'rer,
doomed to spend his life on deck,
takes the bearings of the deep
feels as drowned inside a sack.

✧   ✧   ✧

V

After many false alarms spring has finally arrived, and when the linden trees on the avenue one morning are seen to be in bloom, then it is glorious and impressive and like a festival to wander in the greenish light, which is so kindly to the eye. The air is calm and breathes sheer friendliness, one's foot touches the dry sand that communicates a sense of cleanliness. The fresh grass conceals yesteryear's leaves, muck and trash, much as the first snow does at the end of autumn. The skeletonized trees are filled out, and at last the lofty background of leafy wood stands like a wall of clouds above the shores of the inlet. Pursued by wind and cold in the months before, I can now walk along step by step and, if need be, sit down on a bench and rest. The shore is lined with a row of benches underneath the elms there; and here is where the yellow man, my new-found friend, sits nowadays, with coat unbuttoned, reading his newspaper. Today I discovered—simply by glancing at his newspaper—that we are enemies. And the expression in his eyes, as he read, prompted me to think that he was reading something about me that gladdened his soul, and that he thought that either the poison had been administered to me or was about to be. But he was mistaken; for I do not read that newspaper.

The Major has grown thin and seems worried about the summer. Where he is to spend it is no doubt indifferent to him, but he must leave the city in order not to be left completely alone and feel like a proletarian. This morning he was standing on a point of the shore and seemed to be counting the tiny ripples that were babbling to the stones and pebbles. Simply to have something to do he was striking the air aimlessly with his walking stick. All of a sudden comes from the opposite side of the inlet a trumpet call. He gives a start—and then he sees on the field a squadron of cavalry emerge from behind a hillock, the initial view of it a mass of casks and horse-ears. Immediately after clearing the hillock, the riders come galloping across the field, and shouting and yelling, with sabres clanking, the entire body of men and horses charged forward in military formation. The Major lived his life again, and I could see by the curve of his legs that he himself had been a cavalryman. Perhaps the squadron was one of his old regiment, from which he was now retired, a pensioner removed from his former game. Well—that is the way life is!

Winter and summer, my occult old woman is the same. This winter, however, has placed its mark on her, and she now supports herself with a cane. Moreover, she shows herself only once in a month and belongs to the select few, just as the Queen of the Universe with her dogs.

But with the arrival of the sun and spring, new wanderers have crept into our circle and I look upon them as interlopers. So subtly has the notion of ownership grown in me that I feel as if my morning walks in these parts were my particular and exclusive privilege. I actually look askance at them, for in my self-absorption I have no desire to enter into contact with them through the exchange of glances. This sort of intimacy, however, is insisted upon by people, and they speak with disaffection and indignation about him or her who "does not even look at a person." They seem to feel that they have a right to gaze into and through whomever they meet; but I have never been able to understand from where they derive this prerogative. I sense it as an encroachment, a trespass, a kind of violence to my person; at the very least, an intrusion.

As a young man, I detected that there was a definite difference between persons who fixed their glances on you and those who did not. Today the exchange of glances with an unknown person on the street seems to me to carry the meaning: "Let us be friendly, but nothing more!" But there are some persons whose expressions are challenging, and I cannot persuade myself to enter into this sort of silent compact of friendship with them. All I wish for is a neutral friendship or, if necessary, a hostile one. For a friend always gains a certain influence over me—and that I refuse to tolerate.

Fortunately this encroachment lasts only through the spring, for when summer comes, these strangers depart for the country, and then the streets are as lonely as in winter.

And now the longed-for summer is here. It is here as an accomplished fact and I have grown to be indifferent to it, for I live in my work and in the future. And sometimes in the past, in my memories; and these I piece together, like a child's building blocks. With them I can put together whatever I fancy, and the same remembrance can serve me in every kind of way in one imaginary structure or another, by turning about the blocks with their different colored surfaces. And since the number of groupings and combinations is endless, I obtain an impression of infinity while I play my games.

I have no yearning for the country, but occasionally I feel it as a neglected duty that I do not take walks in a wood, or go bathing in the sea. Added to this, I have a curious sense of shame because of remaining in the city, for spending the summer in the country is considered a prerogative of the social class to which people assign me, even though I place myself outside the pale of society. Besides, I get a forlorn sense of desolation when I realize that all my friends have left the city. While I did not seek them out when they were still here, nonetheless I felt their presence. I could transmit my thoughts to them on a certain street where they lived, but now their tracks have vanished.

When I sit by my writing table, I can discern between the curtains a bay of the Baltic Sea. On the opposite side is the shore with blackish gray cliffs, polished round by the sea waves, and down below, the white water-line. On top of the rocks grows the murky spruce wood. There are times when I am seized with a longing to go out there. But then I merely take my binoculars, and without moving from the spot I am there. I wander upon the pebble stones along the beach, where—among spotlessly clean fence poles, reed and straw,—grow yellow lichen and purple loosestrife beneath the alders. In a crevice of the rock, the fern presses purple-flowered gentian against moss and mushroom, much as ivy does. Some juniper bushes reconnoiter on the edge, and beyond I can see deep into the spruce forest, especially in the evening when the sun is on the descent. There I find pale green open spaces, carpeted with soft liverworts and light underwood of aspen and beech.

Now and then I see something over there that moves, although infrequently. A crow hops about picking up something or other, or makes believe she does, for she gives the impression of being somewhat affected. I notice, however, that she believes herself to be unseen by human eyes. Yet it is certain that she plays the part of the coquette for someone of her own relatives.

A white sloop comes sailing by slowly. Someone is sitting at the tiller behind the main-yard, but I can see only the knees and the elbow. Behind the foresail sits a woman. The boat glides along so gracefully, and when I observe the surging of the sea about the prow, I seem to hear that tranquilizing rippling which, like a sedative, one continually throws off, yet just as often is conscious of—that *something* which is the secret and joy of sailing, except for sitting at the tiller and battling wind and waves.

One day I observed through my binoculars an entire little drama. The pebbled shore over there in the far distance had never yet (except through my binoculars) been invaded by any mortal, and it was my personal property, my solitariness, my summer abode. Then one evening I saw through the right hand lens a flat-bottomed boat come into view. In it sat a ten-year-old girl in a light-colored dress and wearing a red tennis hat. My first thought was: What are you doing out here? But the absurdity of the situation kept me from saying anything at all.

The girl made a neat landing, pulled the punt onto the shore, and then stepped into the boat again and brought out something which glistened at one end. I became curious, for I could not determine what the object was. I screwed up my binoculars a little and saw that it was a small axe. . . . An axe in the hand of a child? The connection between the two was at first beyond my comprehension, and for that reason it gave me the impression as if something clandestine, almost grisly and grewsome, were afoot. First the girl sauntered along the beach, looking for something, the way one does when one is at the shore—looking for something unexpected, something one hopes the unfathomable sea may have left behind. . . . Now, I said to myself, she will begin to skip pebbles. For children can never see pebbles and water without skipping pebbles. Why?—Well, I suppose there is a secret reason for that also. . . . And I was right. She skipped pebbles. After that she climbed up on one of the rocks. . . . Now she will eat purple-flowered gentian, of course, because she is a child of the city and has gone to a public school. (Country children never eat purple-flowered gentian, which city children call common fern, or polypody, or licorice root.)

No, she passed by the ferns and so was therefore a country girl.—She approached the juniper bushes. Now I began to understand—she is going to chop juniper twigs, for it is Saturday, of course.—But no—while she did attempt to take a fling at one of the bushes so that a branch was left dangling, she continued on her way.—She is going to chop wood and make coffee—that's what she intends to do!—No, she kept climbing further up until she came to the edge of the wood. There she stopped and appeared to take measure of the lower branches which had a thick foliage that was freshly green. . . . Suddenly she moved her head, and her eyes followed some object in the air, which—judging by her movements—must have been a bird that had taken flight, for she jerked her head with the same sort of staccato flick that the wagtail uses when it flies, its flight resembling a periodic swoop.

Finally she begins to show what she has in mind to do. With her left hand she takes hold of a branch of spruce and chops off the twigs, tiny, tiny twigs.—But why spruce? Spruce is only used for funerals—and the child is not dressed in mourning. . . . You may argue that she need not necessarily be related to the deceased. Yes, that is true. The twigs are too small for whiskbrooms or to be scattered on the floor of a porch; and in the living-room only juniper twigs are used. But perhaps she is from Dalecarlia, where they use spruce instead of juniper? . . . Well, no matter! —Now something else happens! A few feet from the girl, the lower branches of a large spruce tree are suddenly pushed aside and raised, and a cow sticks out her head and bellows forth a "moo"—I can tell by her wide open mouth and her neck, twisted onto her back. The girl stops short in her intent and her body stiffens from fright. Her terror is so great that she is unable to move. The cow takes a few steps toward her. The child's fear produces a change in current and turns into courage. With raised axe she moves toward the animal, which, after some hesitation and with indignation at having had her friendliness misunderstood, ambles back into her dark hiding-places.

For a moment I had been actually frightened and had made a gesture as if to defend the child; but now that the danger was over, I put away my binoculars, with a reflection upon the difficulty of finding peace.—Think of it! To sit in one's quiet home and be drawn into a drama like this in the far-away distance! And after that I could not stop wondering what the spruce twigs were to be used for!

＊　　　＊　　　＊

My neighbors in the house have gone to the country and I sense that the apartments are empty. I feel as if something exciting has now come to an end. These forces of co-ordination which in the form of husband, wife, children and servants exist in every family, these components of manifestations of the will no longer abide in the rooms; and the house, which always appeared to me like an electric powerhouse from which I derived current, has now ceased to imbue me with strength and energy. I am prostrated, as if all contact with humanity were broken off. All the many little sounds from the various floors stimulated me, and I miss them. Even the dog that awakened me during the night and caused me either to meditate or to fly into a healthy rage, has left an emptiness. The songstress has left a silence after her, and I no longer hear any Beethoven. The telephone in the wall does not sing any more, and when I walk up or down the stairs my steps give an echo throughout the empty floors. It is holiday quiet all through the week, but in its place I hear a ringing in my ears. My very thoughts give me the sensation of being spoken aloud; I feel as if I were in telepathic contact with all absent friends, relatives and enemies; I engage in prolonged, orderly conversation with them, or recapitulate past discussions

60

from our café meetings and other assemblages; I attack their opinions, defend my own viewpoints, and am far more eloquent than before an audience. In this manner life becomes richer and more endurable; it is less wearing, less abrasive, and it does not embitter.

Occasionally this state of mind grows enlarged and then I enter into open hostility against the whole nation; I feel as if people were reading my latest book which is still only in manuscript form; I hear myself being discussed both near and far, and I know I am right, and am astonished no end that they do not realize it. I impart a newly discovered truth, and it is disputed, or the source is made light of, the authority for it doubted, despite the fact that they themselves quote from the very same authority. Forever I sense it as enmity, attack, conflict. No doubt we are all enemies, and friends only when we have to join hands and fight together. I assume that is the way it is meant to be.

Nevertheless this inward life—however vivid and real it may seem—makes me sometimes miss being in touch with life itself. For my faculties, not being in use, ache to be put into action. I wish above all to hear and too see, for otherwise my faculties will from habit begin to operate on their own.

No sooner have I expressed this wish than it is brought to pass. The field in front of my windows begins to fill with troops. First there are infantry-men with gun barrels of metal containing gas-forming elements that, when ignited, hurl out leaden bullets. The soldiers look like sticks split into an angle underneath. After that I see combinations of people and fourlegged animals in motion. That is the cavalry. When a lone rider comes galloping along, his horse makes the same sort of movements as a boat on the crest of a wave; and the rider at the tiller steers, holding the sheet in his left hand. If the squadron, however, should advance in close order formation, then you see a mighty parallelogram of force which from a distance seems to produce the effect of several hundred horsepower.

But the strongest impression is made by the artillery, especially when it competes in a race. Then the ground quakes so that my hanging lamp rattles; and when the men unlimber and fire their guns, the ringing in my ears ceases by itself. Before I became accustomed to this, I felt it as an outrage; but after a few days of firing, I found the reports rather salutary and good for me, for they prevented me from dozing off into eternal rest. And at the discreet distance from which I view these war games, they appear to me like a series of spectacles that are performed for my personal benefit.

❀   ❀   ❀

The evenings grow longer, but I know from experience that I cannot go outside, for the streets and parks are filled with melancholy human beings, to whom a summer in the country has been denied. Now that those, who are economically in better circumstances, have evacuated the city's choicest spots, the poor inhabitants from the outskirts crawl out and occupy the vacated bench spaces. This gives the city an appearance of insurrection; and since beauty is a by-product of wealth, the spectacle is not an attractive one.

One Sunday morning when I felt myself on a level with those in less fortunate circumstances, I decided to tear myself loose and take a drive, that I might get a close glimpse of the people.

I hailed a cab at Nybro (The New Bridge) and stepped inside. The coachman seemed to be sober, but an unusual expression on his face was not conducive to making me feel comfortable. He drove along Strandvägen (The Shore Road), and I noticed a stream of people on the left side while I steadily looked out over the water on the right, over islets and coves, rocks and hillocks, shimmering blue in the distant haze.

Suddenly something happens ahead of us that attracts the attention of the coachman and myself. A large mongrel, with matted coat, looking like a fat wolf trying to resemble a sheep, and evidently the dog of a poor man, keeps pace with the front wheels. With a low forehead, vicious eyes, and so dirty that it is impossible to determine his color, he now and then makes a running jump in an attempt to get up on the coachman's box. One time he succeeds in getting up there but is kicked down by the coachman.

"What sort of beast is that?" I asked in surprise, not only because of the agility of the monster but also because of the bizarre nature of the adventure.

The coachman gave some sort of answer from which I understood that the creature was not his; but when he resorted to the whip, the dog took to the offensive and charged, striving to get inside the cab to me—and this while we were driving at full speed. At the same time I noticed a movement among the crowds of people on the left, and when I look in that direction I discover a procession of creatures that bear some kind of likeness to human beings—all following the contest between the dog and the coachman, and evincing a decided sympathy for the mongrel, who was the offender. On scrutinizing these creatures, I saw that the majority of them were cripples. Crutches and canes alternated with crooked legs and deformed backs; dwarfs with the backs of giants, and giants with the torsos of dwarfs; faces without noses, and feet without toes, terminating in a clod. It was a collection of all the misery that had hidden itself during the winter and now crawled out into the sun in order to have its day in the country. I have seen similar images of human beings reproduced in Ensor's occult larva paintings and on the stage in Gluck's *Orpheus in the lower regions* and thought then that they were fantasy or exaggeration. They did not frighten me now, because I was able to explain their presence and performance; nonetheless it was shocking to witness these hapless human beings, so ill-treated by Fortune, filing past in review on the finest thoroughfare in the city. At the same time I was conscious of a justification for their hostility, which spewed poison over me who was riding in a cab. I was *their friend,* but they were *my enemies!* How strange!

As we drove into Djurgarden, this stream of people was met by a counter-current; but the two mobs passed through and by each other without even a glance, without noticing each other's clothes or faces, for they assuredly knew that they were all of the same ilk, and they kept their eyes focused upon me. Now that I had two lines to pass, I was forced to glance at one or the other side, and I felt sick at heart, and helpless, and was gripped by a longing to see a face that I knew. I reflected how comforting it would be to discern a glance from a friend or an acquaintance, but I found none.

When we passed Hasselbacken, I paid a mental visit there, ascending the steps to the garden and looking around, being almost certain that I would find some friend of mine sitting there.

But now we were approaching the field, and I had a premonition then that there I would unquestionably encounter that certain friendly person. I had a definite feeling that I would! Why, I could not say, but it must have had some connection with a dark tragedy during my youth, which destroyed a family and had an effect upon the children and their fate. How I came to link this tragedy with the Djurgarden field, I cannot say exactly, but it must have been caused by my seeing a hurdy-gurdy with a picture on a metal rod, depicting a murder, perpetrated under horrible circumstances. Although the murdered man was innocent of any guilt, his character was besmirched and he himself blamed for having brought about the murder.

What happens? Why, the man in question—that is, the son, his heir, now turned gray, unmarried and highly respected—comes walking, with his white-haired mother on his arm! Thirty-five years of repressed torture, innocently suffered because of another, had given their countenances that peculiar pallor which is the pallor of death. But what made these rich and respected two take a walk here in surroundings like this? Perhaps they fell prey to that common force of attraction that draws people of the same kind together, perhaps they found consolation in seeing others who had suffered still more, and equally innocently. That I had a foreboding that I would meet them has, I imagine, its secret reasons, hidden deep in the soul—but nonetheless just as persuasive and cogent.

Out upon the open field I now saw new forms of the misery. There came children on bicycles, children eight or ten years old, with malicious expression in their faces, prematurely old little girls with traces of natural beauty, disfigured and distorted by evilness. Even where one saw a handsome face, there appeared an imperfection in the lines, an irregular spacing, a too large

64

nose, an exposure of the gums, protruding eyes that trespassed upon the forehead.

Further on, the mobs thinned out and small groups had pitched camp in the grass. But here it struck me that each group consisted of three persons: two men about one woman—the first act of a pastoral play, ending in a knife slashing tragedy.

At this point the coachman commenced to unbutton his mouth and served me up a few stories. It was not the fact that he was obtrusive that annoyed me, for he did not know any better; what did vex me was that he disturbed me in my thoughts. And when his intelligences about certain ladies driving alongside us forced my attention in a direction where I did not want it to go, I looked upon him as a tormentor and asked him to drive me home.

More saddened than injured by my request, he turned at a crossroad; but at the same moment a cab swung in front of us, carrying two inebriated ladies of a most adventurous appearance. The coachman made an attempt to pass them but did not succeed because of the crush of the throng. Consequently I had to ride behind this coterie; and when their cab was forced to stop because of the mass of people, my cab had to stop also. That gave the appearance that I was pursuing them, and this amused the two ladies no end, and the people on the road as well.

In this manner the gantlet continued, all the way to the city, when I at long last—as after a horrible nightmare—was delivered at the doorstep of my domicile.

"Better then to be alone!" I said to myself; and that was the last time I went out in the evening that summer. Alone in one's own company—which one then had to safeguard in order that it not deteriorate.

*   *   *

And so I remain indoors and enjoy the quietness. I fancy myself being free from the storms of life, wish that I were a little older so that I would not be agitated by the enticements of the world, and believe that I have surmounted the worst.

Then one morning at the breakfast table the maid in the

house comes to me and says: "Your son was here, but I told him you were not yet up."

"My son?"

"Yes, that's what he said."

"That isn't possible! But—what did he look like?"

"He was tall and . . . and he said his name was the same as yours, and that he would come back later."

"How old did he look to be?"

"He was a young gentleman about seventeen, eighteen years old."

I was struck dumb with consternation and alarm; and the girl went out.

There was no end to it, then! The past rose up out of the grave which had been so thoroughly filled in and was now prodigally overlaid with the growth of many years. My son, who at the age of nine, and properly looked after, went to America—and who I thought had found a niche in life! What could have happened? Something unfortunate, or perhaps a series of unfortunate happenings.

What would our reunion be like? That horrible moment of recognition when one looks in vain for the well-known features of the child's face—and for the traits which I myself had helped to implant in him from the cradle so that he might grow up into a fine human being. When dealing with one's own child, one would always try to show one's best side and thus one would see the best side of oneself reflected in this mouldable child's face, which one therefore loved as a more precious, unsullied replica of one's own self. And now I was to see it again, disfigured, defaced; for a youth growing up is ugly because of the irregularity of his features, in which the superman in the child and the awakening animal life of the youth are horribly mingled, with intimations of passions and conflicts, fear of the unknown, remorse over what has already been experienced and tried; and this continuous, unbridled sneering at everything; hatred of all that was oppressive, hatred against the old—consequently against those who had been more favored; distrust of everything in life, it having just changed a harmless child into a predatory human being. All this I knew from experience, and I remember how horrible I myself was as a youth, when all my thoughts, contrary to my will, occupied themselves with nothing but food and drink and crude sensual pleasures.—There was no need for me to see all this again since I was acquainted with it from the past and could not be blamed for it because it stemmed from the demands of nature. And with more common sense than my parents, I had never asked for anything from my son in return. I had brought him up to be an independent human being and had made plain to him from the very beginning what his rights were, along with his duties toward life, himself and his fellow-men. But I knew that he would come with no end of new and greater demands, although his just claims against me had terminated when he was fifteen years old. And that he would sneer when I mentioned his obligations—that I knew also, from past experience.

If what he wanted was merely financial help, it would not be so bad, but even if he disdained my company, he would lay claim to me personally. He would demand the home I did not possess; the friends whom I lacked, connections which he thought I had, and he would use my name to obtain credit.

I knew that he would find me boring; that he would come with views from a strange land, with another way of looking at things, another form of social relations; that he would treat me like an antiquated old rascal without understanding, because I was not a mechanical or electrical engineer.

And how had his character traits developed during these years? Experience has taught me that as we are born, so we remain practically unchanged throughout life. All these many human beings whom I from childhood have seen march through life, have generally retained the same characteristics at the age of fifty, with very slight deviations. A great number had, it is true, suppressed a few glaring attributes which would have interfered with the happy relations with their fellowmen; others had secreted their frailties under a thin layer of veneer; but in substance they remained as they always were. In the exceptions, certain attributes or character traits had come to the fore; in some, these had sprouted upward into virtues, in others, downward into vices. Thus I remember one man, whose firmness grew into obstinacy, whose sense of orderliness became pedantry, whose thriftiness turned into parsimony and miserliness, whose love for humanity shifted into hatred of inhuman creatures. But I also recall one man whose bigotry ended in piety, whose hatred grew into indulgency, whose obstinacy turned into firmness.

✿   ✿   ✿

After having brooded, I went out for my usual morning walk —not to dismiss what was painful but to ponder the inevitable. I thought about all the possible things that might come up during our meeting. But when I came to those questions pertaining to what had happened since our parting, I trembled and began to think of fleeing from the city, even out of the country. However, experience had taught me that the back is the tenderest part of the body and that the chest is protected by formidable shields of bone intended to serve as defense; and so I determined to stay and face the blow.

Hardening my feelings in this manner, adopting the somewhat bare, semi-sarcastic way of looking at things, which is the way of the practical man of the world, I formulated my program. I would put him up at a *pension*, after having first outfitted him, then ask him what he would like to be, promptly find him a position and have him go to work. But above all, I would treat him like a stranger who was to be kept at a distance, indulging in no kind of familiarity or intimacy. And to safeguard myself against intrusion, I would make no allusions to the past, give no advice, allow him complete independence, since he undoubtedly would take no advice anyhow.

This is what I decided upon and determined to follow. . . .

With clear and collected thought I turned homeward, in full consciousness of a change having taken place in my life—a change so violent that the roads, the landscape and the city had taken on a new appearance to me. When I had come half-way across the bridge and looked toward the avenue, I found myself gazing at the figure of a youth—I shall never forget that moment! He was tall and thin and walked with the indecisive steps of one who is waiting for or seeking someone.

I noticed that he, after scrutinizing me, started to tremble, and that he then quickly collected himself, straightened himself up and crossed the avenue, aiming directly for me. I placed myself in a position of defense, heard myself strike a somewhat light-hearted tone as I greeted him with a 'Howdoyoudo, my boy!'

Now that we had come closer and were within a stone's throw of each other, I became aware of his having a distinct mark of *déclassé* about him, of underclass, which I had been most of all in fear of. The hat was not his; it sat on his head as if having been fitted to another's; the trousers did not hang properly, and the bulge of the knee was below the knee itself. His whole appearance had the look of shabbiness—both inner and outer decadence; he resembled a waiter without a job. By now I was able to distinguish his countenance, which was emaciated in a particularly unpleasant way; and now I see his eyes —these large blue eyes surrounded by bluish white. It was he!

This warped, decadent youth was once an angelic child, with a smile that made me reject the whole theory of man's descent from the ape, and the origin of the species; who as a child went dressed like a prince and who had at one time been the playmate of an actual little princess down in Germany. . . .

The horrible cynism of life suddenly became evident to me, but with no trace of self accusation, for I had not abandoned him! . . .

Now we are separated by only a few steps!—A doubt arises in me: it is not he! And at the very same moment I decide to pass by him, leaving it to him to give the sign of recognition.

One! Two! Three!

He passed by me!

Was it or was it not he, I kept asking myself on my way home, firmly convinced that he, under all circumstances, would put in an appearance there. When I arrived home, I called in the maid

69

to question her further, and especially to make certain whether or not the young man whom I had just passed, was my son. But I found it impossible to gain any definite assurance and was held in anxious suspense as long as until dinner time. Now and then I wished that he would appear without delay in order to have it over with; and then again, the situation seemed so trivial, so lacking in reality, that I thought it had ended.

Dinner was over, the afternoon passed, and now I looked at the situation from a different angle that made it appear worse.— He had no doubt believed that I refused to recognize him; and intimidated by this thought he had withdrawn and was now walking about in a strange city, in a foreign country, and had perhaps met up with undesirable companions—perhaps even been brought to despair. Where was I to look for him now? The police!

In this manner I was tormented without knowing why, since I was not the one to prescribe his destiny. And I felt as if a malevolent power had placed me in this false situation in order to lay the blame upon me.

At long last, evening came. Then the maid entered with a card—on which was printed—the name of—my brother's son!

When again I was alone, I naturally felt a certain relief that the now ended peril had turned out to be nothing but a figment of my imagination. But for me this imagining had had the same effect as an actual experience. These fantasies had pressed themselves upon me with an imperative insistence that was irresistible and must have had some primary cause. Perhaps, I said to myself, my son was far away in some strange land and a prey to impressions of the same kind; he might be in distress, in destitution, have a longing to see me—"saw" me, perhaps, on the street, just as I had "seen" him, was torn by the same uncertainty. . . .

With this I put a stop to all broodings and added this happening to the other experiences that I had filed away. I did not dismiss it as something to jest about; I retained it as a precious memory.

The evening was one of heaviness of heart, but tranquil. I did not work, but now and then my eyes would cast a glance at the hands of the clock. At last the time showed nine. With dread I anticipated the last long hour that remained. It seemed to me as endless as eternity, and there was no way to shorten it. My solitude was not of my own choice; it had been forced upon me, and I now abhorred it as a compulsive constraint. I wanted to break away, wished to hear music, something by those great souls who had suffered throughout their lives. . . . I especially longed to hear Beethoven, and I began to bring back to life again in my ear the final movement of the Moonlight Sonata— which for me has become the highest expression of the aspiration for the deliverance of mankind, and one that cannot be attained by any poet!

Twilight had fallen; the window was open; only the flowers on the dining-room table reminded me that it was summer as they stood there in the light, silent, motionless, fragrant.

Then I heard—plainly, acutely, as if from the adjoining room, the mighty presto of the Moonlight Sonata rolling out like a giant fresco painting—I saw and heard it simultaneously; but uncertain whether it was a delusion or not, I was gripped by the kind of shudder which takes possession of one when confronted by the inexplicable. For the music came from the to me unknown benefactress in the house next door—and they were away in the country! However, they could have come to the city on some sort of errand. . . . No matter! The playing was for me; and I accepted the performance with gratitude, with a feeling that I had company in my aloneness and had an affinity of spirit with other children of mankind.

If I now confess that the same allegro was repeated three times during that long, lingering hour, the circumstance seems still more inexplicable. But for that reason it gave me even more pleasure. And that no other piece was played I took as a special favor from above.

At last the clock struck ten, and benevolent, merciful sleep put an end to a day which I shall long remember.

*   *   *

VI

The summer has crept forward to the first of August, the street lights have been lit, and I welcome them. It is fall, consequently time has gone forward, and that is the main thing. Something has been left behind and something is yet to come. The city is changing in appearance; but one can still see a face that one knows, and that is quieting. It invigorates and reassures one. I can even get a chance to talk, and that is something new for me—so new that my voice, from lack of practice, has lowered in register and taken on a suppressed, husky sound, which to me has the semblance of the voice of a stranger.

The firing on the training field has ceased; my neighbors are back from the country and just moving in; the dog is barking again, day and night, and the family's evening gatherings commence anew, their entertainment consisting of a bone being thrown to the other end of the dining room with the dog in pursuit of it, barking ferociously, and growling when the family tries to take it away from him.

The telephone is in action, and the piano playing goes on as usual. Everything is as before, everyone is back, except the Major, the notice of whose death I read in the newspaper this morning. I miss him as one belonging to my circle, but I do not begrudge him his fate, for he had been bored ever since he retired from his army service.

Fall is quickly passing, and the spirit expands with the bracing air, which is easier to breathe. I start going out nights again and wrap myself in the darkness, which makes me invisible. This shortens the evening and prolongs my night's sleep, makes it sounder and deeper.

The habit of converting one's experiences into poetry opens the safety valve for any excess of impressions and compensates for the need of conversation. In my loneliness, experiences are given a semblance of something deliberate, and much of what happens seems to be acted out for my personal benefit. Thus I found myself one evening witnessing a fire in the city, while at the same time I heard the wolves howling at Skansen. These two ends of different ropes were tied together in my imagination, made to have connection, and were woven into a poem, with fitting warp.

THE WOLVES ARE HOWLING

The wolves are howling at Skansen,
out at sea grinds floe against floe,
the pine trees creak on the hillock,
weighted down by Winter's first snow.

The wolves are howling and freezing,
the dogs give an answering bark;
at mid-day the sun is setting,
and soon it is night and dark.

The wolves are howling in darkness,
the street lamps emit their glow
like a midnight sun on the rooftops
of houses clustered below.

The wolves in their caverns are howling,
with a lust for blood in their eye;
they long for forest and mountain
on seeing the fiery sky.

The wolves they howl in their caverns
they howl themselves hoarse from hate;
for as freedom the humans gave them
prison life celibate.

Winds are resting, stillness reigning, now the town clock has
   struck twelve. . . .
Silently the sleighs are gliding, sliding as on polished floor.
Streetcar bells have stopped their tinkling; out of doors no dogs
   are heard.
All are sleeping; lights are out; not a leaf is now seen stirring,
black as velvet hangs the sky, vaulting boundlessly toward
   earth. . . .
High Orion swings his sword, while the Charles' Wain points
   aloft. . . .
In the stove the fire's dead, but afar a pillar of smoke
from an obelisk of smokestack mounts as from a giant kitchen:
it's the baker who at night bakes for us our daily bread.—
It grows higher, rises blue-white; but behold—it now turns red!

Its a fire!
A fire! A fire! A fire!

And a red-hot ball rises up like a moon, like a moon at full;
and the red-hot red turns to white and yellow, spreads out like
   a sunflower bud.
Can it be it's the sun midst the coal-black clouds and the sea of
   houses?
where ev'ry roof is a crest of a wave that is black as a grave?
Now the sky is aflame, every tower and dome in town,
every wire and cable of copper turns red as the deep-tuned
   bass on a harp. . . .
It's neither sun nor the moon! Nor a fire for festive fun!
   It's a fire! A fire! A fire!

But the mountain that lay in darkness is now lighted up and
   shows life;
from their caves the wolves are emitting a howl as if stuck with
   a knife;
out of hate and revenge they are thirsting to burn their oppressors
   and kill. . . .

Just then is heard ringing laughter from the foxhole, a ghastly
   laugh of delight;
in their den, the bears on their heels are dancing, with a grunt
   as of slaughtered pigs.
But the lynx in his lair is silent; one sees only his teeth and his
   glistening grin.

*   *   *

And the seals are wailing their woes! Woe to the city!
Cries as of men being drowned at sea!
And the dogs are all howling in chorus;
they whimper and yelp and bark,
they tug and tear at collar and chain,
weep and whine and make sounds
like spirits, tortured and damned!
They—they alone, the dogs, have compassion with us,
with their friends the human beings. . . .
What a sympathy!

The elks are now waking, the princes of North woods,
they gather and stretch their longlegged shanks,
take a trot and a tumble inside their pen,
fenced in by a railing.
They keep bumping against the fence poles
like birds against panes,
and, bewildered by their hurts,
they wonder whether day has now dawned—
a day again like all the others,
deadly boring and long
without any other palpable aim
than to be turned into night. . . .

And now the birds come to life in their cages!
The eagles are flapping their wings;
screeching, they vainly try to soar,
strain to fly upward into space;
striking their heads against iron bars,
they bite the grating, clawing and clanging,

75

until, exhausted, they fall
into the dust and lie crippled,
with dragging wings, as on bended knee,
begging, pleading for mercy—
for a gift of grace
giving them back the air in space
and their freedom.

Like feathered arrows, the falcons dart
hither and thither whistling;
the buzzards are moaning
like ailing children. . . .
The tame wild geese have come awake
and with distended necks produce
a tuneful chord of herdsman's horns.
The swans are mutely swimming,
snapping at tongues of fire
mirrored between floating flake and floe
and, like goldfish, dart to and fro
on the pond's surface;
then they stand still and stick their heads down
into the blackish water . . .
the white swans bite themselves fast
in the mud at the lake's bottom
lest they be forced to see
how the heavens burn up. . . .

It's dark again. The fire siren
has signaled calm throughout the town and land;
a cloud of smoke is stretched above the city,
shaped like a giant's black, enormous hand. . . .

❈   ❈   ❈

My communion is nowadays restricted to the impersonal
through my reading. Balzac, whose fifty volumes have been my
companion during the past ten years, has for me become a personal friend, of whom I never tire. True, he has never brought

forth what people—especially in these days—call works of art, art being often confounded with literature. Everything about him is artless; one is never aware of the construction, and I have never been conscious of his style. He does not play with words, never poses with unnecessary images or figures of speech—which, by the way, belong to "poetizing"—yet he has such a distinctive sense of form that the content is always given the clarity of expression that is exactly covered by the word. He disdains all show and has the same effect on you as a story teller at a gathering, who now gives an account of a happening, now brings in the characters to speak, and occasionally makes comments and explains. For him everything is history—*his* history of contemporary times. Every little individual is shown in the light of his own generation, but his origin is given as well, his development under this or that form of government—all of it widening the mental horizon and the range of observation and placing a background behind every character. When I think of all the senseless, foolish things that have been written about Balzac by his contemporaries, I am struck dumb. This truthful, trusting, forbearing man was in the schoolbooks of my youthful days called an uncharitable physiologist, a materialist, and so forth. Yet still more paradoxical is the fact the physiologist Zola paid homage to Balzac as his great teacher and master. Who can comprehend this? And the same situation can be ascribed to my other literary friend, Goethe, who in recent times has been utilized for all manner of purposes, most often for the ridiculous exhumation of paganism. Goethe, as we know, has many different stages upon his path of life. By way of Rousseau, Kant, Schelling, Spinoza, he arrives at a view-point of his own, which might be termed the philosophy of enlightenment. He has solved all questions; everything is so simple and clear that a child can grasp it. But then comes the moment when pantheistic explanations of the unexplainable are found to be wanting. Everything seems to the septuagenarian so strange, so singular, so unfathomable. It is then that mysticism comes into evidence—and then none other than Swedenborg is made use of. Yet nothing is of any avail, for in the second part of FAUST he surrenders to the force of the

77

Almighty, reconciles himself to life, becomes altruistic, devoting himself to bog-reclamation, and turning half socialist, and is apotheosized with all the apparatus of the Catholic Church pertaining to the teachings of the last Judgment.

The Faust of the first part, who in his wrestling with God has emerged like a victorious Saul, turns out to be a defeated Paul in Part II. This is my Goethe! Yet, although each person has his own opinion, I cannot understand where one finds the pagan, unless it be in a few mischievous verse fragments in which he lashes out at the ecclesiastics; or perhaps it could be in PROMETHEUS, where the fettered son of the gods might be meant to denote the Crucified One (Jesus) scoffing at the rejected Zeus.

No, it is the whole of Goethe's life, and the poetry based on it, that appeals to me. It was an older friend of the poet who during Goethe's younger years gave him the key to his authorship. "Your aspiration, your rightful aim, is to give a poetic picture of life as it is; the others have sought to externalize the so called poetic, the imaginative, but that leads to and creates nothing but stupidities."

In this way Goethe himself relates it in one of the pages in his "Aus meinem Leben"; elsewhere in the same work he says: "And so I commenced in that direction, from which I could never swerve, namely to transform everything that gladdened or pained, or in some way engaged me, into poetic or scenic form, both for the purpose of setting right my own conceptions of reality and to bring order and tranquility to my soul. No one was in greater need of this gift than I, whose nature tossed me continuously from one extreme to another. Consequently everything I have written has been pieced together from one single great confession and whose fulfillment is this book (Aus meinem Leben)."

The charm of reading Goethe consists for me in the light touch with which he makes his impact. It is as though he could not comprehend life in absolute earnest, whether because it is lacking in firm reality, or does not deserve our grieving and our tears. In addition to this, the absence of fear with which he approaches the divine powers, to which he feels an affinity; his disdain for formality and convention; his want of ready-made opinions; his steady growth and rejuvenation, through which he ever remains the youngest, always in the vanguard, ahead of his time.

Always in the past and to our present day Goethe is referred to as the antithesis of Schiller, and the two have been fabricated into an either/or relationship—exactly as was done with Rousseau and Voltaire. I cannot subscribe to this alternative, for I can find room for both because they are complementary to each other. I cannot in words describe the differences between them, not even perfunctorily, for Schiller has more feeling for form, especially in his dramatic works, and he takes wing and soars as high as Goethe. The development of both is a concerted effort, for they exerted an influence upon each other. Thus there is room for both where they stand on a single pedestal in Weimar; and since they stretch out their hands to each other, I see no reason for separating them.

✿   ✿   ✿

Winter has come again; the sky is gray, and the light is reflected from below, from the white snow on the ground. The solitude synchronizes well with the suspended life of nature, but occasionally it becomes too oppressive. I long for fellow human beings, but in my loneliness I have grown as sensitive as if my soul were stripped of its skin; and when it comes to exercising control over my thoughts I am so spoiled that I find it hard to tolerate coming into contact with another person. Indeed, every stranger who approaches me, suffocates me with his spiritual and intellectual atmosphere which, as it were, encroaches upon my own. But one evening my maid entered with a visiting card at the very moment when I yearned for companionship and was in a mood for receiving no matter who, even the most unsympathetic caller. At the sight of the card I was elated, but when I read the name on it my joy turned into cheerlessness, for it was the name of a total stranger.—Never mind, I said to myself, it is nevertheless a human being!—Let him come in!

A moment later a young man entered. He was very pale, very hesitant, so that I could not determine to which social stratum

79

he belonged; so much the less since his attire did not cling to the contours of his body. He was, however, exceedingly positive and self-assured, yet held himself on the defensive, playing a waiting game. After having paid me a few compliments, which acted as a damper on me, he went directly on to his errand and asked for a loan. I replied that it was against my principles to lend money to a complete stranger, because in the past I had often given help to the wrong person. Just then I discovered that he had a red scar on his forehead, above the left eye, and at this very moment it appeared blood-red. Simultaneously the man took on a grisly aspect to me; but the next moment I was grippd by compassion for his profound misery, and contemplating myself in a similar situation I had a change of heart. In order not to prolong his agony I handed him some money and invited him to sit down.

As he pocketed the money, he seemed more surprised than grateful and acted as if he would like to leave, since his errand had been completed. I began by inquiring from where he came. He looked at me with astonishment and stammered forth: "I thought that you were familiar with my name." He said this with a certain pride that was offensive to me, and when I confessed my ignorance, he uttered, quietly and with dignity:

"I have been in prison."

"In prison?"—At this moment he became interesting to me, for I was just then in the throes of a criminal story.

"Yes—I had pocketed twenty crowns which did not belong to me. My employer forgave me, and all was forgotten. But then I started to write for another newspaper—I am a journalist, you see,—an article against dissenters; and then the matter was raked up again, and I was prosecuted."

This was an awkward case. I felt myself being almost challenged to say something, yet was reluctant to do so. I fended off the thought and detoured.

"Well—can such a thing, in our 'enlightened' times, prevent a man from getting work—because he has been a con . . . ?"

The last word was clipped off by a disparaging expression on the young man's face.

To mend matters I suggested to him that he write for a very democratic newspaper whose editor I knew to stand above the prejudice that a man who had served his punishment could not be redeemed in the sight of society.

When he heard the name of the newspaper, he gave out a disdainful snort and answered:

"That's the newspaper I am fighting against!"

This seemed to me completely preposterous, for I thought that in his present position he would seek the one support open to him for rehabilitation. But as the circumstances were muddy and I am averse to wasting time trying to solve matters of this sort, I detoured again, seized by the very human desire to obtain a service in return. And now I shaped my question in a jovial, friendly tone, devoid of any prejudice.

"Well, tell me now, is prison life really so hard? What does the actual punishment consist of?"

He looked as if he considered the subject an indiscreet intrusion and as if his feelings were hurt.

In order to help him, I did not wait for an answer, and so I went on:

"I assume it is the loneliness. . . ." (Here I gave *myself* a stab—but one does that quite often when one has a compulsion to speak.)

Drudgingly he picked up the ball I had thrown and retorted: "Yes, I am not accustomed to solitude, to being alone, and have always looked upon it as a punishment for people who are evil." (There! There I got it back for stretching out my hand to him, and I felt it as you would when bitten by a dog that you try to stroke! But I don't think he knew that he bit me!)

A pause ensued and I noticed that he had punctured himself, and that it made him irate, for he had not had me in mind when he gave expression to the feelings of a man relegated to solitude.

We had now run aground and had to come afloat again. Since my position was actually the more enviable, I decided to free him from his excommunication and to descend to his level so that he would leave with a feeling of having received something other than money. But I did not understand the man; I suspected that he looked upon himself as innocent and a martyr, victim of a reprehensible action on the part of his editor.

Yes, he seemed to have forgiven himself and to have evened the score already at the first settlement,—the crime had been committed by the other party when this man started proceedings. But the young man must have felt in the air that he could not count upon any support from my side; and the whole time we spent together seemed to be marked by a grave miscalculation. He had had the impression that I was a different person; perhaps he had also observed that he had commenced at the wrong end and that it was too late to change.

Consequently I took a new tack and spoke, as I thought, words of enlightenment and wisdom, to make him think that I had noticed his discouraged spirit and apprehension of his fellowmen.

"You are not going to let yourself be defeated by this. . . . (I purposely avoided the word.) The age in which we live has advanced to the extent that it finds that . . . that an expiated punishment (here the young man made a frowning face again) . . . has been atoned for and erased. Not long ago I sat with some friends at Hotel Rydberg. In our company was a former comrade who had served two years in Langholmen Prison. (I intentionally did not choose my words with delicacy.) And none the less he had been guilty of serious forgery."

Here I stopped for a pause in order to observe some lightening of his countenance which I expected to see reflected from within. But he seemed only to be offended and irritated that I should have dared to place him, who was innocent and had been wronged, in the same category as one who had served time in Langholmen. But a certain curiosity could be seen in his eyes, and when I, by an abrupt silence, forced him to speak, he asked curtly:

"What was his name?"

"It would be wrong for me to say, since you do not suspect who it is. However, he has written down and has published his impressions of the prison, without trying to defend his indefensible crime; and because of this he has regained his former position and his friends."

This must have struck him like a blow, even though it was intended as a pat on the shoulder; for the man rose, and so did I, since there was nothing more to say. He took leave of me like a gentleman; but when I caught a view of his back and noticed his drooping shoulders and dragging feet, I became almost afraid of him. For he belonged to that group of human beings who seem to be thrown together out of incongruous, unmatched pieces.

After he had departed, the thought occurred to me: Perhaps what he told me was nothing but a fabrication.

And after having scrutinized his visiting card, on which he had written his address, it suddenly struck me that not long ago I had seen that same handwriting in an anonymous letter. I brought out the box in which I keep such letters and began to look for it. This is something one should never do, for while I was hunting for *his* letter, all the others filed before me . . . and I suffered as many heart stings as there were letter writers.

After having gone through the pile three times, being certain that I would find his handwriting there, I gave up, persuaded by a distinct impression: "You must not delve into his destiny! But give help you must, without questioning. You know best why!"

The room had taken on a different atmosphere; the stranger had brought with him something heart-sickening, and I had to go out into the open. There must have been something tough and tenacious in his spirit, for I was obliged to move the chair on which he had been seated, lest I still see him sitting there after he had gone.

And so I went out, after having opened the window—not to let out any material odor but to air out an impression.

❖   ❖   ❖

There are ancient streets that are lacking in atmosphere, and others that are new, which have it. The most recent extension of Riddargatan (The Street of Knights) is filled with roman-

83

ticism, not to say mysticism. You see no one there; no shops deface the buildings, the street has distinction, is hedged in and deserted, even though the large houses enclose so many human destinies.

The names of the great figures of the Thirty Years' War at the cross-streets add to the overpowering impression of history, past ages blending fascinatingly with modern times. When one turns the corner of Banérgatan one sees to the west at Grev Magnigatan a slope which serpentines inward to the right, providing the perspective with a mysterious terminus, and imparting to it a shadow. within which anything conceivable could happen.

If one approaches from the west, however,—the ancient part of Riddargatan—and looks down toward Grev Magnigatan, the bend in the street is very sharp, and the palatial-looking houses with their dark-colored façades, their portals and towers, testify to fortunes and destinies of unusual magnitude. There live today tycoons and statesmen who exert an influence upon nations and dynasties. But immediately above, toward Grev Magnigatan, stands a surviving old house from the beginning of the past century. This house I like to pass, for there is where I lived during my stormy youth. There plans were made for campaigns which eventually were carried out successfully; there I wrote my first important literary effort. It is not a bright memory, for the poverty, the humiliations, the unsettled conditions, and the dissensions placed a stigma upon it all.

This evening I felt a longing to see this house once more, without knowing why. And when I found the old unhappy house again, it stood there looking just as in the past. But now it had been plastered, and the window arches had been freshly painted. I recognized the long, narrow entrance leading to the backyard and resembling a tunnel with its two gutters, the entrance door itself with its iron bar, supporting one of the doors, the doorknocker, the small signboards advertising ironing, glove cleaning, shoe repairing, etc. . . .

As I stood there in thought, a man, walking with a brisk step, came from behind, putting his arm around my neck as only a very old acquaintance will do, and asked: "Are you on your way up to your old home?"

It was a young man, a composer, together with whom I had worked one time, and with whom I therefore was well acquainted.

Without any ado I followed him into the house, up the wooden stairs, and—lo and behold!—we stopped two flights up, outside my own room!

When we had entered and he had lighted a candle, I sank thirty years back into time, and I actually saw again my bachelor quarters, with the same old wallpaper but with new furniture.

And when we had seated ourselves, I felt as if *he* were visiting *me*, and not the other way around. Yet, there was a grand piano, and so we immediately started to talk about music. But the man was—as is the habit of most musicians—so completely occupied with his music that he scarcely could or would speak about anything else. He was so detached from the age in which we lived that he knew nothing about it. When I mentioned the words *riksdag*, cabinet member, Boer War, strikes, or the right to vote, he kept silent, without seeming to be either disturbed or annoyed by the subject or by his ignorance; for to him the subject simply did not exist. And even when we discussed music, he merely touched upon it generally, without attaching himself to any opinion. For him everything consisted of tones, measures and rhythm, and the spoken word was used by him to bring out only what was necessary in daily intercourse.

I was aware of this, and so I needed only to point to the open piano and he would sit down and play. And when he began to fill the ugly little room with the strains of music, I felt myself within a magic sphere, in which my present consciousness was obliterated and my other one from the 1870's reappeared.

I saw myself lying in the sofa bed which stood precisely at the spot where I now sat, before a nailed up door. It was on one night. . . . I woke up by hearing my neighbor, who had his bed on the other side of the door, restlessly turning and twisting, sometimes sighing and moaning. Being young, fearless and selfish, I merely exerted myself to fall asleep again. — — — — The

85

time was then only twelve, and I was hoping that my neighbor had merely come home inebriated.

At one o'clock I was awakened by a cry for help—and I thought it was I myself who had cried out, for I was just then having a nightmare. No sound was heard from the neighbor; it was absolutely silent in there. But something disagreeable emanated from his room; a cold current of air, a watchful eye riveted on me, as if someone in there were listening to me or peering through the keyhole to observe what I was doing.

I could not go back to sleep. I kept fighting against something, something ghastly, something awful. Now and then I wished that I might hear a sound from within. Yet, although we were separated by only a foot, I heard nothing—not even a breath or the rustling of the bedlinen.

At long last, morning arrived. I got up and went out. When I returned home, I learned that my neighbor, who was a foundation-work contractor, had died during the night. I had therefore been lying next to a corpse.

(While I was seeing again this whole scene, the music was going on, and I continued to go over my memories undisturbed.)

The next day I heard the preparations being made for the laying out of the body and for the funeral; the clatter of the coffin on the stairs, the washing of the corpse, the old women's subdued prattle.

So long as the sun was up, I found this only interesting and was able to joke about it with those who came to see me. But when darkness fell and I was left alone, I felt that inexplicable iciness which radiates from a dead body, coming into my room —an iciness which is not a lowering in temperature or an absence of warmth but a positive, freezing coldness that no thermometer registers.

I had to go outside, and I went to a café. There I was jeered at for being afraid of the dark, and so was persuaded to abandon my resolve to sleep somewhere else and returned home, somewhat under the influence of a few drinks.

A shudder came over me when I went to lie down again next

to the corpse, but I nevertheless crept into bed. I cannot explain it, but the dead body seemed still to possess some faculties of life which put it in communication with me. Through the door emanated what seemed an unmistakable odor of brass, coming straight into my nostrils and robbing me of sleep. A silence such as is peculiar to death only pervaded in the beginning throughout the house, and the dead contractor seemed to have greater power over the living than he had while alive. Through the thin double flooring and the walls I heard later whispers and murmurs from sleepless beings long past midnight. After that, contrary to what usually happened, the house grew completely silent. Not even the policeman, who was in the habit of getting up to report for his night beat, was heard.

I heard the clocks striking one, two. . . . And I jumped out of bed, awakened by a din from where the corpse lay. I heard three knocks! Three! I immediately thought the man had merely been thought to be dead, and I had no desire to be witness to any ghost walking scene, so I seized a handful of clothes and raced down one flight, where an acquaintance of mine lived. I was received with appropriate banter and allowed to rest on the wooden cover to his bed.

That was the first time I began to ponder the everyday phenomenon of death, which is so elementary and yet exerts such a mysterious effect upon even the most lighthearted.

(My friend at the piano, no doubt affected by my reveries, had held to the more somber music but now changed and passed over into something very gay and bright.)

The fulness and power of the tones forced me, as it were, out of the cramped room and I felt an urge to throw myself through the double windows. I therefore turned my head and projected my glance upon the pianist from behind; and as there were no shades, it skipped outside and across the street into a flat in the house on the opposite side, whose height was lower, and so I found myself stealing in on a little family in the midst of their evening meal.

There I saw a plain, lithe young woman moving about a dining table, at which a four-year-old boy was seated. On the table stood a vase with chrysanthemums: two large white ones, and one that had the color of a yellow flame. I stretched forward and observed that the table was set and that the boy was about to have his dinner. The young woman fastened a napkin under his chin; and when she did this, she leaned forward so deeply that the back of her head was completely exposed, and I saw a little neck, delicate as a flower stalk. And the lovely little head, with its abundant hair, bent down like a flower bud over the child, shielding, protecting. The boy at the same time made one of those engaging dual movements of the head, first a backward one to allow room for the napkin, then a forward one, pressing down the stiff linen with his chin so that his mouth opened wide, showing his white milk-teeth.

This woman could not possibly be the mother, for she was much too young, nor could she be the boy's sister, for she was too old for that; but she was undoubtedly related in some way.

The room was plain but neat. It had a number of portraits on the walls and on the mantelpiece of the porcelain stove, bespeaking a love of family; and crocheted antimacassars lay on some of the furniture.—Now the young girl sat down at the table —luckily not to eat; for to look at anyone eating when one does not eat oneself is ugly. She sat down in order to keep the child company and to beguile it into thinking the food tasty. The little boy was not in good humor, but the 'auntie' (I already called her that) soon persuaded him to smile, and I could tell by the motion of her mouth that she was singing to him. That I *saw* her song without hearing it, while at the same time my pianist was playing, struck me as being so very mysterious. But I thought that he was accompanying her, or that he ought to be. I was in both rooms simultaneously, but primarily in the room across the street, and I acted as a bridge between the two, as it were. The three chrysanthemums seemed to me to be participants in the play, and I felt for a moment their healthful, healing camphor odor blending with the innocent fragrance from her hair, and this drew the interest away from the food on the table, obliterating it, so that the child appeared to open his mouth only to breathe sweetness and to smile at his beautiful comrade at table.

The white milk glass upon the white tablecloth, the white chinaware and the white chrysanthemums, the white stove and the white faces—everything was so white in there, and the young girl's maternal feelings toward this child to which she had not given birth, shone like a white light when she now untied the napkin, wiped the little boy's mouth, and kissed him.

At that same moment my pianist turned in the direction of the street and I noticed that he was playing for her; and I realized that he had seen her . . . and throughout had been conscious of her presence there.

I felt myself superfluous and in the way, and so I indicated that I wished to leave. But he insisted that I remain, and we ended the evening by making an agreement to join efforts in a new work.

*　　*　　*

VII

I went back to my pianist friend, both because I had regained my youth at his abode and because we were now engaged upon a new work together. That I also enjoyed his music I did not consider to be a misappropriation, for his music was not for me but for her.

Many an evening I witnessed almost the same scene in her room. Everything was much as before: the child, the napkin, the glass of milk; only the flowers in the vase took on a new appearance—yet they remained chrysanthemums. However, they were different in that the third blossom bore another color. But the two white ones always set the fundamental color tone. Were I to put my finger on the secret of the young girl's charm, it lay more in her movements than in form; and her rhythmic action seemed to be in tune with his music. Yes, one would have thought that he composed to her tempo, her dancing steps, her undulating walk, her expressive arms, fluttering like wings, the arching of her neck.

We never spoke of her, made believe we were not aware of her. Yet we lived her life, and I noticed one day that I had embodied her in the music for my drama.

This would not have been a cause for regret, in the event that she had fitted into the play with my heavy-hearted thinking. But that she did not, for her soul moved in $3/4$ measure and it always terminated in waltz. I was disinclined to mention this to my friend, for I knew that by alluding to it with even one word, the enchantment would be broken and that if he had to choose between her and me, he would have chucked me.

❖   ❖   ❖

This winter had crept forward quite pleasantly for I was no longer alone, and I had a goal for my wanderings hither and

90

thither. Besides I felt as if I were living some kind of family life when I took an interest in a woman and a child.

Spring came early, already in March.—One evening I was sitting at my table, writing, when my pianist friend was announced and was shown inside. By the light of the lamp I saw the mild little man approaching me with a mischievous look on his face, and holding in his hand something which he wished to give me.

It was a card. I took it and read two names on it: a man's and a woman's. He was engaged to her. As we by this time scarcely needed to speak, I answered merely with a smile and spoke the one word: "Chrysanthemum," accented by a question mark. He answered with an affirmative nod of the head.

The matter appeared to me to be quite natural; it was as if I had known it forever. Therefore we exchanged no words about it; instead we talked about our work together and then said good-bye to each other.

I was tormented by no curiosity, for I knew the answers to any questions as yet not asked. How they had met?—The usual way, of course. Who was she?—His betrothed. When did they intend to get married?—In the summer, naturally. Of what concern was it to me, anyhow? Yes—there was the risk that she might interrupt our common work—and which I found only natural—and that my evenings together with him might come to an end all at once. This would only be a logical sequel of the great event, although he said—when he stood in the doorway saying good-bye to me—that he would always be at home to me every evening at seven-thirty and that, in case he was not at home when I came, to go inside and wait; the key I would find on top of the cabinet in the hall.

I let three evenings pass, and on the fourth I stepped out about half past six to see whether he was possibly at home. As I was climbing the stairs, it occurred to me that I had failed to glance at his window, as one usually does, to see whether there was a light in his room. At the door I fumbled in vain for the key, so I took the one lying on the cabinet, where I thirty years before used to find it, and went inside—exactly as in those days in the past—and I was now back in my old room.

It was a strange moment, for I fell immediately back into my youth, felt the whole of the unknown future pressing upon me and lurking in ambush for me, was conscious of the self-intoxication of prospects and advance payments, certainty of victory, and downheartedness, overestimation of my talent, and underrating of my own ability and efforts.

Without lighting the lamp I sat down on a chair, for the street-lamp—the same street-lamp that had shone on my misery—cast its frugal light inside and silhouetted the cross of the window frames on the wallpaper in the shadows.

There I sat, and had behind me all, all, all! The struggle, the victory, the defeats! All the bitterest and the loveliest that life can give. And just the same? What—what then? Was I old and tired? No! The struggle was still going on, angrier than ever, more serious and on a still greater scale, forward, ever forward; but if I had previously had enemies before me, I now had them both before me and at my back. I had been resting in order to be able to go on; and as I now sat in this sofa in this room, I felt myself just as young and capable of fight as I did a generation ago. The only difference was that the goal was now a new one, since the old milestones had been left in the distance. Those who had remained and lagged behind tried, of course, to hold me back, but I could not wait; therefore I must walk on alone and explore the wildernesses, seek new paths. Sometimes disillusioned by a mirage, I had to turn back and strike a retreat, yet not further back than the crossroads—and then proceed forward again.

I had forgotten the window that had no shade, and when I suddenly came to think of it I got up. I beheld in the house on the opposite side precisely what I had been expecting.

There he sat now at the chrysanthemum table. She sat beside him, and both were occupied with the child, which was neither his nor hers. The boy was her nephew, the only child of a widow. That their first love was given to and concentrated in a child gave to their relationship from the beginning something of unselfishness, while at the same time it ennobled their feelings which found a meeting point in an innocent little being. And it occurred to me that he had gained a security for himself through her already developed instinct for motherhood.

Now and then they would regard each other, forgetting the child, and whenever they did, they did so with an indescribable expression of bliss, such as two human beings, when alone, take on when they meet and avow to fight against loneliness by themselves. Besides, they did not even seem to be thinking of anything at all, neither of the past nor the present, but lived only for the moment, rejoicing in being near to each other. "To sit at a table and look at each other as long as life should last!"

Happy that I had come as far as I had, now that I could find joy in the happiness of others, without any trace of feeling of loss, or imagined apprehensions or misgivings, I left the torture chamber of my youth and returned home to my solitude, my work, and my struggles.